BEDROLLS, BUSHES ᴬⁿᴰBEACHES

THE HIPPIE YEARS

RON WHITE

ISBN: 978-1-5136-4225-3

Published by: Flower Power Press

FOREWORD

It's that moment when you involuntarily draw a breath as your mind spins toward clarity. "Oh wow, really? Now I get it," I said when Ron shared with me the details of his horrendous childhood and suffering from unspeakable abuse.

I began to understand my friend, who is widely admired for his world travels and exploits. He had not been running towards exciting places, but instead, away from unspeakable cruelty. The revelation came decades later.

My first recollection of Ron was seeing his fiery mane on Storybook Drive, adjacent to the Belair Shopping Center in Bowie. I was driving my car when I spotted a coterie of well-entertained friends gathered around him. "Who is this," I thought, "cavorting on a sidewalk with them in the middle of nowhere?"

This began the often-told tale of Ron's ban from the shopping center and the subsequent hilarious court appearance, which follows in this wonderful book, *Bedrolls, Bushes and Beaches*.

I am proud to be a part of Ron's antics, of which there are many, such as his expulsion from high school commonly misunderstood at the time only to be discovered later as a 'honor' reserved mostly for the brightest among us.

Ron and I were at Woodstock, traveling separately although our Bowie friends managed to find each other. What a coincidence. I saw Joe Cocker perform *With a Little Help From My Friends*. How appropriate. I remember Joe Cocker and two guitar players. I heard singing in beautiful falsetto voices. Where was this coming from? To my amazement, the voices belonged to the guitar players. I almost missed Woodstock because I had to study for exams. I'm glad I made the right decision.

Once I was among friends, waxing lyrical about the time when an Allman Brothers concert was sold out and being turned away at the gate was imminent. Ron said, "Wait here," and a few minutes later, the door opens, and there is Ron instructing the doorman, pointing, "Yes, those two right there," and miraculously we found ourselves inside. If that ending wasn't exciting enough …

But wait, as I finish, someone in the group adds, "I had the exact same experience!" At first, you feel annoyed and wonder if it is BS until you stop to think for a moment and conclude to yourself, "That's Ron!"

One of my fondest memories with Ron is our witty banters, and how we cracked each other up in the best of the 'old days'. Yet, behind the mask of laughter and wit, there was always the shadow of abuse which, by his energetic and hilarious antics, he successfully disguised to his friends for decades.

My friendship with Ron spans 50 years. A friendship that, despite his troubles and perhaps because of them, was paramount to my attempting to become a better human, and it continues to this day.

I spoke with Ron after each of his trips. It was tempting to hit the road with him although my priorities lay elsewhere. I believe everyone has a friend who is a tour de force. You're about to read some unbelievable and astonishing times of my best friend, Ron.

Michael McHale

Bowie, Maryland, October 2018

A WORD OF THANKS...

I would like to express my sincere gratitude to all the good Samaritans who assisted me and others whose names I do not remember. A special mention to my coach, TC Cummings and Harvey Sroloff.

This book is dedicated to the love of my life,
my wife Jill.

TRACK LISTING

SLEEVE NOTES

In September 2017, the final stop of our five-week European tour was Amsterdam. My wife Jill and I intentionally saved the best for last, and this city was our grand finale. The 'fun' capital of Europe was the most fitting conclusion to our extraordinary vacation.

It was forty-eight years since my last visit to Amsterdam. My departure as a young man was abrupt due to unfortunate circumstances, and this only propelled my desire to return someday. I had no inkling it would be five decades later. When I reminisce about Amsterdam, it was the happiest and unhappiest of times.

At nineteen, I was lost and searching for direction. My dream was to work my way around the world, with 'work' being the operative word as my unlikely journey began with $15.00 in my pocket. These were the days when credit cards were rare, and cash was the primary form of payment. Oftentimes, I had the equivalent of $1.00 or less when thousands of miles from home.

Nevertheless, I prevailed, and my dream to circumnavigate the world came true. My success was attributed to hard work and creativity, coupled with tremendous help and kindness from remarkable human beings I met along the way. The people, the places, and the songs of the time all had significant roles in the soundtrack of my formative years. The photograph on the front cover was taken as I left home to hitchhike to Woodstock.

For many of us, the music of our youth was predominant in helping form the memories we treasure today. We all have favorite playlists of our most beloved songs, and I wrapped my memories around mine in a way to share with others.

In the chapters to follow-or tracks as I have called them-you will learn how my yearnings to see the world came to fruition through my adventures on the open road. They were primarily outlandish escapades coupled with tragic loss. These circumstances meant travel, in addition to my dream, was the cure to heal my broken soul and rebuild my crushed spirit.

Two special people we met at the beginning of our European tour lit the spark for chronicling my adventures, and as I reclined in my seat next to Jill on the flight home from Amsterdam, further memories were rekindled. I recounted a few thoughts on a piece of paper and from those words, this book was born.

There are multiple modes of transportation when I am going to a new country. This time, I climb into the thin narrow metal tube filled with people in rows of seats and offer a "Good day to you," to my seatmate as I sit down.

This metal tube was possibly a coffee can in a previous life and now it has powerful engines attached. The acceleration increases, thrusting my body into the seatback, and I am firmly planted. With the build to lift off, the maximum forces are dynamically aligned, propelling us towards our next destination. The buildings, cars, roads, and people below slowly shrink in size. It is magical; fear, anxiety, frustration, and stress disappear.

I unbuckle my seat belt, and I am free to move around the cabin. In a few hours, I will enjoy another new culture, food, beverages, and people. I recall the beautiful, tingling feeling which is normally only felt during lovemaking.

I step out of the metal tube and walk towards the concourse. I am bombarded with the images and sounds of new surroundings. Hearing languages I cannot understand, the passengers flow in many directions, unlike the daily routine of monotonous work life. The masks of deception await certain folks at baggage claim. They appear naked, lost, and confused.

Many others frantically surge towards the exit. They boldly push forward by any means necessary to return home, the same place they could not wait to leave. Oh, the dichotomy of it all. Other people browse souvenir shops and snack bars, taking a respite, watching the ebb and flow along the concourse.

I navigate obstacles along the way. Small IEDs disguised as suitcases, swinging purses, backpacks on amateurs, human projectiles exiting lavatories, lost in thought and intent on rejoining the human chain to their way station called the luggage carousel.

There are legions of faces, glazed with anticipation or overwhelmed with fear. Their routines disrupted, as they are confronted with instantaneous decisions.

The perpetual movement of humankind, devoured in the bowels of an airport, streams towards several types of metal transport contraptions. Taxis and buses await transiting passengers. The masses of friends, relatives, spouses, siblings, children, and parents, all peer nervously at the faces jostling through the doors wondering if their loved one will arrive before a police officer writes a ticket.

The enticement of travel is a welcome invitation ... onward to the next destination. As I exit the airport, exhilaration courses through my body.

To your safe travels ...

Ron

Ron White
New York, October 2018

The baby in the bathtub is surrounded by warm water as his mother caresses him. The warm water covers his head as he sinks lower to the bottom of the tub with his mother's hands on his shoulders. Is it time for sleep? The baby gurgles in unison with the water flowing into the bathtub and then naps as the teenage mother lays unconscious on the floor.

TRACK ONE

PETER, PAUL AND MARY: PUFF (THE MAGIC DRAGON)

We all have dreams, the things we desire most in our lives, and some of us are successful in accomplishing our goals. I am fortunate to have achieved one of my early dreams. My aspiration to travel was first formulated when I was a young lad, and since then, this has been my life's work. My travels are ongoing to this day, and this is how it all began.

I sat in my elementary school classroom, thinking of faraway lands, as I stared, somewhat attentive to the teacher, at the world globe displayed prominently on the right corner of her desk. I often fantasized of the wonders, delights, and adventures awaiting the wandering traveler. The schoolroom windows became movie screens, offering glimpses of the wildlife and beauty of Africa or smiling hula dancers, welcoming me with their flower leis. Such daydreams were a diversion from the mundane lessons of the day.

My first journey of note occurred in December 1961. My father was hired at the U.S. Government Printing Office in Washington, DC, and we moved from Syosset, Long Island to Bowie, MD. Situated between Washington, DC and Annapolis, MD, Bowie was described as an idyllic town, and in some ways, it was. The new tract homes were close to Washington, DC, the heart and soul of the U.S. political world, and this was my new environment as I reached puberty.

As a precursor to my later happy times in foreign lands, in Bowie, I was excited yet bewildered to be among strangers rather than old friends and relatives. I navigated a new culture very different from my former neighborhood. The lovely, freshly-painted homes with manicured lawns which were occupied by middle-class Americans with expanding families as they re-established their lives after World War II. It was a mini melting pot of cultures, a fine blend from all around the U.S. and other places.

A new community sprouted from practically nothing to become a vibrant, bustling city, as William Levitt built house after house on the 2,300-acre Belair Estate he purchased for $1.75 million. The original colonial plantation belonged to the Provincial Governor of Maryland, Samuel Ogle and then his son Governor Benjamin Ogle. James T. Woodward, an affluent banker, purchased the estate in 1898, and his nephew, William Woodward, Sr., heir to the Manufacturer's Hanover Bank fortune, inherited the property in 1910.

This estate was sold to Levitt in 1957 following the death of William Woodward's son, Billy, who was shot by his wife Ann because she believed he was a burglar. *Life* magazine described the tragedy as the "Shooting of the Century".

The first stage of building began early in 1961, and this new community had limited services, stores, and schools. Consequently, I traveled to Upper Marlboro, MD sixteen miles away for junior high school. The Upper Marlboro area was the original Marlboro country and a major grower of tobacco.

My dream to travel was nurtured when I became a *Washington Daily News* paperboy at age 12. The headlines emblazoned across the front page screamed for attention as they described tragedies and momentous events from home and around the world. I was shocked by the untimely deaths of Marilyn Monroe and John F. Kennedy, and of major achievements such as astronaut John Glenn orbiting the Earth.

This was my introduction to the world beyond my home and family, as local and international news facilitated my slowly expanding learning curve, allowing me to move beyond my parents' grasp. At an early age, I came to the realization that my parents were incompetent and wholly unprepared to raise children. They barely managed their own lives.

My newspaper route plus odd jobs including shoveling snow, mowing lawns, selling Amway and Fuller Brush products provided a reprieve from the daily abuse at home. I withstood the worst types of mental and physical abuse that are criminal today, punishable by life imprisonment. Behind closed doors, it is known only to the victims. The damage is oftentimes catastrophic, and this, beyond my simple yearning to see far-off lands, was an equal motivation for travel.

I was unaware of what was happening within the immaculate homes of Bowie. The weekday morning routine of fathers trooping to work in their carpools to return in the evening. The smiling faces of happy children carrying their books as they traipsed to school in the early morning hours. It was a tranquil setting to raise a child in the secure confines of home, away from the dangers lurking in cities, but there was a dark underbelly.

I did not discover until years later that my neighborhood friend Carol was being sexually assaulted by her grandfather. John, whose family lived around the corner, and his siblings were beaten and abused by their alcoholic father. Sadly, the list goes on, and these isolated incidents were not rare. Fortunately, most of us survived, although the challenges were greater for some.

From a young age, I desperately searched for a method to regain my lost soul. This was my world, and surviving my parents was my childhood. The list of their offenses is long, but irrelevant now, other than this formed the initial foundation of my life. Who I am today is all based on my childhood.

Could I blame my parents? Yes, however, I chose not to take that route. They are sick, and you may even consider them mentally deranged. I could also blame the lottery of life that placed me with not one, but two disturbed parents. My ability to persevere the confrontations became a lifesaving education.

As an unwanted child, I was not loved by my parents, and I accepted this fact. I was the undesirable result of their youthful lust and subsequent obligatory marriage. I adapted to this alien existence by imagining my future. During my teenage years, my subscription to National Geographic magazine helped build my knowledge of a beautiful world simply a plane ride away. Peace and tranquility were attainable, so I thought.

My job was to reach adulthood before casting off to somewhere else. My mind conjured the excitement of faraway lands and customs. I voraciously read biographies of famous individuals, internalizing their thoughts and achievements in overcoming life's obstacles. I applied kernels of their wisdom as my invisible life preserver. I discovered the importance of laughter and fun regardless of physical and emotional pain.

Also, I developed an uncanny strength to confront unseen internal foes within myself. Some of my friends also faced their own hidden internal enemies. Most of them successfully dodged life's attractive fatal mistakes. As a teenager, my struggles intensified with larger challenges when I least expected them. Of course, in hindsight, it all makes sense now. My harsh lessons became valuable tools later in the game of life. To me, life is the most thrilling sporting event.

My initiation in the proverbial boxing ring occurred at Frederick Sasser junior high school with Tommy, who became my nemesis in 1962. One of my 8th grade classmates was 16-year-old Tommy, the class bully, who weighed 150 lbs. and stood 5'11" tall.

The reason for his incomparable size versus everyone else in the class was he failed the three previous school years. He was infamous in school; his entourage carried his books and admiringly listened to his reform school exploits. My physique was the opposite of his, a skinny 13-year-old Jewish redhead from New York with a weight of 75 lbs. and a height of 4'5".

The ultimate clash of our worlds surfaced on the day of the annual mock 'slave auction', a major activity of the school year. On the big day of the auction, the entire student body gathered in the auditorium where half a dozen popular students were auctioned to the highest cash bidder. The new 'slave owners' included hormonally charged girls, who bought a slave for the day. The auction rules required the slave to be obedient and accompany their owner everywhere for the remainder of the day.

The auction ended when the school bell sounded, and students dispersed to their various classes. I was the last student to enter the metal shop classroom, and Tommy's perception of me as the carpetbagger interloper, encouraged by the idea of slavery, fueled his wrath. He defiantly blocked the path to my desk and grinned proudly with resolve to crush his enemy before the teacher's arrival.

As I approached Tommy, my diminutive size necessitated craning my neck to be face to face with him. Tommy's partners were behind him, glued with blood lust to witness the demise of a Yankee. His arrogant, ever-widening smile lit a fuse in my core, and it was up to me to defend the virtue of the North.

My reply to his ever-broadening arrogant grin was an awe-inspiring punch to his stomach. His cheeks resembled every artist's impression of the face of the wind blowing in the clouds, as the air rushed from his lungs. If I was taller, my preference was to hit him in the face, and I, too, was surprised by the might of my punch. I imagined the cartoon caption 'kapow!' above his head.

Tommy's stupefied expression was priceless, and my timing was perfect. The school bell rang to signal the start of class, and Tommy and I, he still somewhat bent over, went to our desks. After class, I heard students continuously whispering in disbelief "Ronny socked Tommy!" I became a man with one punch.

Five years later, Tommy was on death row at the Maryland State Penitentiary for murder—the ultimate end of the line for all bullies—and I had become the archetypal hippie hitchhiker.

On the floor in my bedroom, the magic carpet waits for lift off. The carpet can fly, I was told. I did not believe it at first. Now I am convinced because it was shown on TV.

My magic carpet has all the major conveniences, including a well-stocked pantry, stove, shower, and toilet. This is a luxury carpet. The salesman did not exaggerate.

My magic carpet flies high in the sky. People on the street below resemble my toy soldiers. The skyscrapers are tiny dots on the landscape.

Soon I will be somewhere exotic. I believe in a land called Honahlee where only daring souls venture. Next stop, Honahlee!

TRACK TWO
THE 5TH DIMENSION: AGE OF AQUARIUS

T eenagers living in the 1960s faced a far different world than the teenagers of today. During the decade when John F. Kennedy entered the White House, change was coming. The fabric of American society was unraveling, and a full-fledged cultural rebellion was underway by the late 1960s. The counterculture celebrated personal freedom at the expense of traditional social mores, and youthful rebels defied parental authority and officialdom.

It was under this framework of social upheaval when, on January 1st, 1967—a mere five months before I was to graduate high school, at the age of 17—I was forcibly committed to a mental hospital. Allegations were made by my parents as they engineered my incarceration, claiming I was an uncontrollable child. They stated I hit my mother. When completing their affidavit seeking my committal, they failed to mention I was three years old at the time. Such was the extent of our adversarial relationship. The legal proceedings which placed me in the State's custody occurred in a juvenile court, and I was not allowed to defend myself or be represented by an attorney. I was merely a piece of unwanted property.

In 1949, I became a member of the Baby Boomers who were born into the world. My younger sister and brother arrived later. It was a chance meeting poolside between my parents at a resort hotel in Wurtsboro, NY. Following their weekend tryst, my mother became pregnant. My 21-year-old father and 17-year-old mother chose marriage. They were emotionally and mentally unprepared to raise a child. This was my unwelcome entry into the world.

My parents constantly fought with each other, and I became the scapegoat for their problems. The dysfunctional nature of their interpersonal relationship led to my receiving the brunt of their collective anger. My parents accepted the misguided advice from their marriage counselor that my presence was required in their sessions. It was my refusal to attend their marriage counseling sessions which led to my commitment to Spring Grove State Mental Hospital.

As my father's threats of arrest escalated due to my noncompliance with his demands, I foolishly believed he was bluffing. My father was adamant. My world crumbled the day of my arrest. The first phases of adult life are typically college, career, and marriage. These concepts became as foreign to me as living on another planet.

Unfortunately, my father believed the marriage counselor's recommendation that incarceration may "scare me into submission." This, in a nutshell, was the older generation attempting to crush youthful rebellion.

"You're under arrest," said the burly police officer.

"I've done nothing!"

"Sorry son, but this warrant says otherwise. Now hold out your arms, and let's do this without trouble."

I submitted as he snapped on the handcuffs and then stepped into the back of the police car. I was angry and very scared.

As we drove through the streets of Bowie, I sank into the depths of this horror. My parents' betrayal torched my soul. My frenzied mind foresaw a flaming fire as I was consumed. I was not a child to be loved and cherished, but a tasty char-broiled morsel of lunch tossed to the hungry crocodiles of the State's mental health apparatus for them to voraciously rip the flesh from my bones. I clutched for a shred of sanity.

My expectation was to be released momentarily, ending this injustice. As I fought to calm myself, I did not foresee the magnitude of the damage to my psyche my dysfunctional parents caused when they absolved their responsibility of me and I became a ward of the State of Maryland. The doctors eventually concluded I was a normal seventeen-year-old, and reform school was too severe a punishment. The detailed evaluation period to reach this conclusion lasted three months.

The process was thorough, and I was given a clean bill of mental health, but these experts never expressed compassion at my erroneous incarceration. I was not the first or the last innocent lamb to be sent to the slaughterhouse. Their professional objective was to identify the root cause of 'the problem', one way or another. Since there was none, I and others around me were living our own *One Flew Over the Cuckoo's Nest* experience.

The sixties were an era of growing enthusiasm for new psychiatric drugs. It was also the time of ECT-electroconvulsive shock therapy—and the hospital used this in an assembly line technique to administer a 'cure' for homosexuals and other so-called deviants. I witnessed the devastating effects of the treatment firsthand. The alleged cure inflicted serious harm and left patients babbling husks of their former selves. For what? I asked myself. Beyond the moral ramifications, there was also the practical matter of my own survival in this environment.

In the U.S. in the mid-1960s, psychiatric institution residents were moved to local mental health homes or similar facilities, and this meant a larger proportion of the remaining incarcerated residents were prone to violence. It was a common occurrence for bored patients to quarrel and fight. On Saturday night, two days before I was due to be released, a patient I nicknamed the Strangler accosted me in the hallway.

He was 25 years old, 6'1" and weighed 200 pounds versus my age of 17, height of 5'11", and weight of 120 pounds. His intimidating physique resembled a typical collegiate football player, plus he was the undeniable bully of the ward. In the preceding weeks, I had read an insane person has five times the strength of a sane person. I wanted to avoid confirming this fact firsthand.

With his gang of misfit followers and admirers, perhaps I should have called him Tommy. He walked the ward with this cohorts marking his territory like an alpha dog. The Strangler was always accompanied by four other lunatics, all of them termed 'lifers', violent troublemakers and murderers whom doctors considered to be hopeless cases, without the possibility of being released. The day I overheard him brag how he strangled his brother to death led to this descriptive moniker.

The Strangler and his entourage adhered to their own 'rules', and punishment by the authorities was not a deterrent. The standard penalties for misbehavior were solitary confinement, transfer to a higher security building, ECT, or stronger doses of medication. Unfortunately, these consequences did not prevent their wanton acts. It was simply another day on the funny farm for them.

On the Saturday evening before my planned Monday release, I exited the day room, and the Strangler initiated his attack while his cohorts watched with glee. My reaction was instinctive, and I swiftly retaliated. After a flurry of punches and swings, somehow, I managed to wrap my left arm tightly around his neck. I was surprised by his distraught, fearful face for a split second before he regained his composure. His entourage was in disbelief by my immediate success in thwarting his brazen onslaught as the orderlies rushed to stop the fight. I was the evening's entertainment for the Strangler and his gang, with an outcome they did not expect.

The next morning, I had forgotten the fight and was in a carefree mood as I relaxed on my bed, awaiting my release the next day. It was my

Sunday routine to escape the madness of the ward since this was the only day we were permitted to remain in our rooms. The rest of the week we were restricted to the recreational room or the hallway, where usually half a dozen 'pacers' wandered. These men were generally the most troubled of the patients, rarely speaking, and smoking cigarettes endlessly, as they paced the hallway all day.

I thumbed through an edition of *Motor Trend* magazine as I anticipated my release, scheduled for 9:00 a.m. the next morning. The expectation of continuing my education, going to college, and resuming a normal life elicited cheerful thoughts. It was a partly cloudy winter's day, and everything was bright as I immersed myself in the glossy pages, seeking to ignore the insanity beyond my room. I was anxious to be released to recommence my studies and work, proud of my achievements thus far in both.

My parents informed me at six years old that it was my responsibility to pay for college. This marked the start of working odd jobs. My stock portfolio was established at age thirteen when the shares purchased were primarily based on wild hunches. I amassed stock shares in Levitt and Sons, Toyota, and Xerox, and was gratified by the robust performance of these companies. Combined with my odd jobs of delivering newspapers, mowing lawns, and shoveling snow, I had ample savings to begin college by age seventeen.

My primary psychological savior in the corrections facility was monitoring my small portfolio which steadily increased in value. My investment growth some weeks exceeded a doctor's salary, and my impatience to be free was all-consuming. Freedom became my mantra, and later in '67, I vowed to avoid haircuts after I heard of the musical *Hair*, in which freedom and peace are said to have ushered in the Age of Aquarius.

As I read a review of the new 427 Cobra—with a top speed of 164 mph—the Strangler and his cohorts strutted into my room. I was now faced with a final exam for insane asylum survival, and hoped the adroitness learned from often dodging my raging mother and violent father could be instrumental in saving my life. I rose from my bed and stood by the wall.

This 'visit' was the last thing I expected before my departure, and now I regretted being in my room alone. My sights were set on my release; last night's fight was history. However, it was clearly on the Strangler's mind as he happily smirked, his face so close to mine I could smell his bad breath.

He grabbed my toothbrush, put it in his mouth to cover it with his saliva, and then stomped on it. As far as I was concerned, it was an old toothbrush. His tactic was met with my stone-cold expression and silence. This response infuriated him and triggered his wrath.

He cheerfully wrapped his hands around my neck with the speed of a professional wrestler, and I was caught off guard. The five to one odds were not in my favor. The safest option was to remain calm; he had four lunatics on his side, anxious to see my bloody body on the floor. I was lifted off the floor effortlessly by his huge, capable hands. Was Humpty Dumpty set to have a permanent fall?

Although smaller than him, my rage and anger were equal to his, regardless of his physical advantage, and my first instinct was to attack; my second was to remain calm. He strangled his brother, and now I was in an identical plight. Stall for time. I lost hope as my ability to successfully escape this predicament rapidly diminished by the second.

This bloodthirsty brute was fixated on his prey, as I was a few inches over his head being held by my neck. My body and imminent death hung in the air, at the hands of this madman. After fifteen long seconds, he lowered me to the floor and turned his attention to his friends. The Strangler's next tactic was to enlist his gang to help murder me. After they huddled together and discussed the murderous plan, he gave them the order.

"Let's do this; we can kill him and say we are crazy." He had a good point.

The plot unraveled when he noticed one of his buddies closed the door when they entered the room. There is one handle on the outside, and patients are unable to open the closed door from the inside. Through the small glass window in the door, the Strangler yelled to one of the pacers to open the door. My greatest fear was one of the pacers unwittingly opening the door, allowing the Strangler and his accomplices the opportunity to escape after my murder.

It was evident I was involved with the Five Stooges, and it was morbidly comical—another *Cuckoo's Nest* moment—as the Strangler tried to convince his comrades this murder should be a group undertaking, and it was time to revise the plot. The Strangler now directed his attention towards dismantling my bed, while I remained frozen. While he was engrossed in savagely ripping my bed frame apart, I breathed a small sigh of relief and believed there was a chance to escape with my life.

The Strangler speedily destroyed the bed frame and a piece of bedpost snapped free, fitting firmly in his large, beefy hands. The plan involved murdering me and escaping. My immediate fear was the Strangler breaking the small window in the door sealing my fate.

He lifted the bedpost to smash the glass window, and it was poor timing on his part since an orderly came to investigate why there was more than one person in the room. (I later heard this was brought to his attention by one of the pacers.) Just as the orderly's face appeared near the window, the bedpost crashed through it, and the startled man jumped back sharply. The Strangler narrowly came close to killing two people.

The fuming orderly stormed into the room, demanding the culprit who broke the window. No one uttered a word. The orderly threatened 24-hour solitary confinement for all of us. This was my ticket home since I had only twenty-two hours before my release. It was the safest way to ensure my survival. Jubilant, I had won the day and the rest of my life.

The patients always shout, "You'll be back!" upon anyone's release, but it was the last time I saw them. In the morning, I ambled outside breathing freely which led to the first smile in some time. My improved state of mind imploded the next day when I sought to enroll in a high school in Baltimore and my worst fears were validated.

My three-month absence from school required repeating 12th grade, and my life was forever altered; all my plans were destroyed. My dreams slipped away like ice cream in the sun. My classmates graduated and embarked on the next chapter in their lives, while I was a fish out of water fighting for my life.

As a condition of my release, I lived in a halfway house in Baltimore for five months. During this period, I worked as a clerk at the Maryland Commission on Interracial Problems & Relations and at the Baltimore Gas & Electric Company. I also purchased items at local auctions to be resold to conventioneers at the nearby civic center. I was on the slow road to recovery.

On my eighteenth birthday in June, it was time to register for the U.S. military's draft system, designed to enroll young men in the armed forces, with the high probability of combat in the Vietnam War. Enlisting in the U.S. Navy was also a possibility when I celebrated my coming of age and registered at the local draft board in Baltimore. I was drowning and grasping at straws. The disagreements with my parents remained and dealing with them was worse than a war in southeast Asia.

This was the same time Muhammad Ali refused to join the U.S. Army and this development was extensively reported in the news, especially when he was stripped of his world title. In my high school years, the Vietnam War was a daily news event as the war raged. The easiest way to obtain an Army deferment was by attending college. Muhammad Ali's religious attempt to avoid the U.S. Army was a more difficult option.

This was 1967, and American troops serving in Vietnam further increased to 475,000 as the peace rallies multiplied and the number of protesters opposing the war grew. Among those serving were *some* of my friends, who shunned college and joined the Marines and the Army. I discussed my thoughts of enlisting in the U.S. Navy with these friends who advised not to do it. Nevertheless, I perceived military service as an escape, providing a possibility to travel.

Contrary to the advice of my peers, I decided to enlist and completed the enlistment process and passed the physical. I was handed the necessary papers, and the sergeant said, "Come back tomorrow with these papers signed and then you'll go into the U.S. Navy." That night, I had second thoughts and chose to wait. It would be wiser to graduate high school first.

While in Baltimore, the other important event on my eighteenth birthday was achieving my dream to buy a new car. I bought a brand-new 1967 Ford Mustang. Other options for me at the time were the Pontiac Firebird, Mercury Cougar or the 427 Cobra I'd read about on that almost fateful morning. Chevrolet had plans to roll out their new Chevy Camaro muscle car, but the new and more powerful Ford Mustang was the only car for me. In my mind, I believed the car might somehow drive me to recovery.

In the interim, I visited dealerships in the Baltimore and suburban areas in Maryland and found the best price was from a dealership located two blocks from the halfway house—I paid a little more than $2,700. This amount has a value today of a little less than $20,000. Consumer goods were a better value in the '60s when the Federal minimum hourly wage was $1.40 and a gallon of gas cost 33 cents.

I was in nirvana with my new car purchase, and it was the happiest day of my life. As the keys were placed in my hands, the pain from the previous months dissolved. Years of hard work and investments had paid off, allowing me to attain one lifetime goal. The day I drove the car from the dealership to visit my friend Ernie in Bowie, I passed the halfway house with a big smile on my face and a rare feeling of euphoria. I was on the open road without a care.

If you like Mustangs, the classically designed '67 is more stylish than the others. As I rest my hands on the smooth steering wheel, the interior sparkles with a new instrument panel layout, and more luxurious hardware. Man, I'm in heaven as I shift into first gear and, after passing the halfway house, I head towards Bowie.

In another magazine I read—the November 1966 issue of Car and Driver—people said the bigger engine in the Mustang is equivalent to dropping an anchor and overloading the front end. It doesn't, and the balance and handling are superb.

Will I leave the past behind in my exhaust trail? I waited for this moment, and now it is here. I stop at a traffic light and see a strange expression from an old lady on the sidewalk. I grin broadly, and I wave to her. "Don't worry about me. I'm an alien from another planet!"

The light turns green before she can cross—perhaps she wanted to stand there and admire my car—and I ease away with a growl sending shivers down my spine, but I'm not cold. I slide the climate control to MAX A/C and feel the compressor hum. Cold air roars from the vents, and the outer world fades into oblivion as I crank the handle and close the window.

I twist the dial on the radio to another station, and soon I'm singing along to Junior Walker and the Allstars' (I'm a) Road Runner—how appropriate. I imagine the driver in the next lane is listening to the same station as he mouths the words to the song. He's driving an old Chevy and also appears happy with the freedom of the road.

As I drive on, I spot a guy with his thumb out and slow down to pick him up, but a pickup truck stops first and gives him a ride. I'm slightly disappointed. He was young like me.

I increase the volume to drown out my thoughts. I'm happy today, yet my moods swing easily. I'm joining the Navy? No … it doesn't feel right, and I'll see next year. Will I obtain a draft deferment and go to college? What will I study? Right now, I don't care.

I consider detouring to Annapolis; no, onward to Bowie. My resistance to delay is due to my nervousness to see Ernie for the first time in six months. He's a good buddy, but he will have questions.

"Of course, he'll be cool!" I say out loud. This is my day.

The miles go by, and the trees are a blur from the window as bugs are squashed on the windshield. Forward and onward to my destination, the past is behind me, and I will peer into the future. Those bugs are my past life and experiences, and I'm driving towards high times.

My parents firmly believed their decision to have me arrested was helpful, and our troubled relationship was now beyond repair. In September, filled with dread, I returned to their house in Bowie to attend night school. The yearning to run away and avoid the challenges ahead was overwhelming. I felt my education was more important. Anonymity in the household was my earnest endeavor.

I was welcomed home by my parents, and the arrest was never mentioned, but being there was tough, and my relationship with them was barely tolerable. It was a daily struggle to calm the avalanche of fears disrupting my thoughts and concentration. The cause and effect from the previous traumatic incidents in my life became a vicious cycle. I did my best to cope, reminding myself this would not last forever, and an illusion of normalcy was achieved by smoking hash and drinking.

I attended night school yet remained overly concerned with unforeseen events which might derail my plans for college and the future. Home life was under a 'conditional love' mandate, an arbitrary parental guideline for love and punishment—love is exhibited only when secret conditions are met.

By visiting friends, dating girls, and partying, I spent less time at home when not embroiled in my busy schedule of working, attending night school, and studying. During the day, I worked as a U.S. postman which required me to purchase the uniform. Despite the modicum of freedom in the outdoors, the job was boring and lasted six months. After I quit the Postal Service, the uniform was the most expensive piece of clothing in my closet.

TRACK THREE

OTIS REDDING: (SITTIN' ON) THE DOCK OF THE BAY

On January 30th, 1968, under what became known as the Tet Offensive, the North Vietnamese launched a coordinated series of attacks on more than 100 cities and outposts in South Vietnam. The purpose was an attempt to foment rebellion among the South Vietnamese population and encourage the U.S. to scale back its involvement in the Vietnam War. Though U.S. and South Vietnamese forces managed to thwart the attacks, news coverage of the massive offensive stunned the American public and increased support for the anti-war movement.

As this new offensive unfolded, respected TV journalist Walter Cronkite, who had been a moderate and balanced observer of the war's progress, announced it seemed "more certain than ever that the bloody experience of Vietnam is to end in a stalemate." For me, this heralded further 'proof' I made the right decision not to join the U.S. Navy.

More violence filled the news later in the year, with the assassination of Robert Kennedy and the shooting of Andy Warhol. While these events were disturbing, I had two major personal accomplishments in June of '68. The first was my high school graduation, and this was a tremendous boost to my confidence. It was time to leave home to start college at Prince George's Community College, and then one of my friends mentioned a nice apartment available near campus. The rent was affordable with my savings and part-time work.

As my life regained a semblance of order, the backdrop for the country remained in growing turmoil. The second Kennedy assassination was preceded in April with the death of Martin Luther King, and August ushered in the Democratic National Convention riots in Chicago. As the Vietnam War protests escalated inside and outside the Convention Hall, the U.S. perspective was severely polarized by the Soviet Union and communism.

This U.S. perspective was one of defiant disapproval after the end of World War II. To stop the spread of communism, the government's policies dictated intervention in the affairs of countries it deemed susceptible to communist influence. This led to our involvement in Vietnam—at a cost in excess of two million Vietnamese and nearly 58,000 American lives.

Democratic Convention delegates from across the country were split on the question of Vietnam. A faction led by anti-war Senator Eugene McCarthy challenged the long-held assumption that the U.S. should win the war at all costs. The debate intensified to the extent of physical fights on the convention floor, where delegates and reporters were beaten to the ground.

The delegates for the status quo, championed by then Vice President Hubert Humphrey, won the day, although the events of the convention severely hurt the Democratic Party. This led to the loss of the Presidential election to Richard Nixon. The debate raged inside the hall, while several thousand anti-war protesters gathered on the streets of Chicago to show their support for McCarthy and demand the withdrawal of troops from Vietnam.

Chicago Mayor Richard Daley deployed 12,000 police officers and requested another 15,000 state and federal officers to contain the protesters, and the action then rapidly spiraled out of control. Police severely beat (and gassed) demonstrators and journalists, and some attending first responders. The police action caused the deaths of eleven people and the arrests of over two thousand.

In September '68, I began my first semester of college at Prince George's Community College. I majored in Business Administration and, based on my previous investment success, I aspired to become a successful stockbroker on Wall Street.

In December '68, Apollo 8 launched and orbited the moon, but I missed the news broadcast as I sailed with my family from Miami to Key Largo. This winter holiday was a test for the possibility of reconciliation with my parents after I moved into my own apartment. The close quarters on the boat only magnified the schism between me and my dysfunctional family. I sat on the bow, the furthest point away from my parents.

My father's plan was to sail the boat round trip from Miami to Key Largo; mine was to jump ship the second we docked in Key Largo on December 27th. As I hurried along the dock, my father yelled, "Be at the Miami marina parking lot at noon Sunday for the ride home!" The marina in Miami was where my father's boat was to be docked for the winter and where the family car was parked. One thousand long miles back to Bowie in the car with my parents; this was a thought I wanted to avoid for now.

As I disembarked the boat, a surge of adrenaline erupted. I embraced the freedom of being ashore and away from my parents. With $3.00 in my pocket, my next stop was Coconut Grove, a popular place for teenagers, hippies, and backpackers, not far from the Miami marina rendezvous.

The three-day *Monterey Pop Festival* was a key part of what was proclaimed as the 1967 'Summer of Love', which coincided with the year of my eighteenth birthday. A cultural revolution was in full swing on the streets of the Haight-Ashbury district in San Francisco; similarly, music blared, and drugs were shared in Miami too. This phenomenon happened in the earthy artist village of Coconut Grove before the upscale shops, hotels, condominiums, and cafes arrived in the 1980s and later. In the sixties, it was a hippie hangout.

The dock and sailboat were forgotten as I hitchhiked on the Overseas Highway, discovering the pleasure of hitchhiking in the Keys. The passing traffic was mostly cars, and I saw a few eighteen-wheel trucks, traveling at 70 mph or higher. The bane of every person who raises their thumb; the dirt, dust, noise, and wind are a nuisance, the equivalent to a mini sandstorm every minute or so. Their absence was a teaser for the future. The freedom of the open road liberated my soul, and a travel addict was born.

There are few towns in between Key Largo and Miami, and it was a single ride as most vehicles traveled to Miami. I arrived within two hours, and I was not disappointed with Coconut Grove. It was a hippie paradise at Peacock Park, a mirror of what was happening in San Francisco. The sound of music emanated from strumming guitars, and the aroma of marijuana permeated the air. There were peace signs, long-haired, shirtless young men and euphoric, dancing women wearing tie-dye dresses. This groovy site became my home for now, as thoughts of the rendezvous with my family receded into the background.

I roamed Miami Beach later and assessed my needs for the upcoming days. I left Key Largo with a small backpack containing only shirts, socks, and a toothbrush. I located a secluded spot to sleep near the marina rendezvous, but it was a frigid night, and the light coat I wore provided little warmth. The gradual buildup of cold chills culminated in uncontrollable shivering, disrupting my slumber every fifteen to twenty minutes.

Sitting on the dock in the early morning hours, I watched the seagulls and waited for the warm sun. Stray dogs and cats finished their night of scavenging and searched for a refuge to rest. It was incredibly peaceful by the sun and sea, with a gentle, prevailing wind. Although the ghosts of my past lurked in the background, I'll dream for now in Miami.

The sunrise ushers in a new day. The power and warmth of the sun's rays rise as their intensity increases throughout the day. The sun is a tiny speck on the horizon as it emerges in the morning, yet in minutes, it transforms into a huge globe which commands the sky and the universe.

It is a good day to walk along the beach. In my bare feet, I stroll and admire the beauty of the palm trees swaying in the gentle breeze. The ocean tide recedes and then advances to my feet, softly cleansing as I stroll. I am impressed this powerful ocean offers a comforting embrace.

As the seagulls fly above my head, I dance past the now increasing intensity of the incoming tide. My energy is limitless like the sun's; perhaps in four billion years I will be tired.

I am a passenger on this planet, and it is a wonderful world with plenty to do and an abundance of choices offered every day. Today, I choose to walk alone along the peaceful beach, and the soothing sand warms my feet; it is an enchanting sensation. The gentle breeze cools my body as the temperature rises, and I am free to wander; the possibilities are infinite.

"All aboard," I hear in the distance and envision the unbelievable sights and destinations in store. "Wait for me," I yell as I run in the sand. Now it is harder than I imagined, and my weight coupled with the velocity adds to the difficulty in movement. With every step, the sand rises higher and higher.

I open my eyes. This is a different world. Where is the airplane? My theme song is blowing in the wind. My

*world is suddenly turned upside down. I stare blankly at
my watch. The second hand is motionless. I examine my
surroundings and slowly comprehend the world which lies
beneath the sand.*

The warm sun soothed my cold bones as I returned to Coconut Grove
in search of breakfast. In a small café, a coffee and donut were served
by a lovely waitress with a bright smile.

"Where were you last night when I was shivering?" I asked.

She laughed and asked, "Are you going to the festival?" as she poured
the thick black liquid into a white china mug.

"Festival?" I questioned, my interest immediately piqued.

"Sure, honey. There's been a bunch of hippies like you comin' through
here this week."

"Is there some kind of music festival?" I asked, my heart beginning to race.

"Miami Pop Festival or something," she replied. "Wait a minute."

She brought the coffee pot to its stand and then handed me a poster that
was propped in the window. I missed it when I walked in.

"Here, honey. Have a look," she said.

To my amazement, I was thrust into a real-life mind-blowing dream
come true. My wish to attend a music festival was answered. The poster
listed the bands and dates, beginning in a few hours. This revelation
explained my deliverance to Miami.

With my coffee cooling, I studied the details and noticed the roster
contained many of the most popular bands of 1968. I was living a
dream, flabbergasted by the fortuitous and uncanny luck of the day
and the kind nature of the mood-enhancing waitress.

Then reality slapped me in the face—I was due to meet my parents at midday. My dismay lasted only seconds. I slapped reality back as an ever-broadening jackpot smile, similar to my waitress', spread across my face. Although it would cause my parents some consternation, the decision was simple: skip the rendezvous at the marina parking lot and attend the Miami Pop Festival.

I gulped the coffee and hustled to pay the cashier after replacing the poster in the restaurant window. I sprinted to the side of the road to hitchhike to the festival. I would avoid the sand for a few more days.

TRACK FOUR
STEPPENWOLF: THE OSTRICH

The *Miami Pop Festival* was my first music festival, with others to follow in upcoming years. This was also the first major American rock festival east of California with two concurrently operating main stages, both featuring talent of equal caliber. It was the first to be widely publicized to—and draw crowds from—areas beyond its host state.

The promotional campaign for the festival covered the entire eastern and midwestern U.S., as far west as Texas, and north into Canada, introducing the concept of the pop/rock festival into a truly national— and accessible—phenomenon for the first time. It was a significant milestone to help spread the counterculture movement nationwide in America.

This was the second of two festivals, both with the same name, to be held in 1968 at Gulfstream Park, a horse racing track in Hallandale, Florida, a little north of Miami. Apart from the venue, the two events were not related. The first of the two festivals occurred in May, and the event I attended in December was originally publicized on promotional materials as the *1968 Pop and Underground Festival* and the *1968 Pop Festival*. This later came to be referred to colloquially as *The Miami Pop*

Festival, a practice which led to widespread confusion between the two events which had different promoters.

Of the many bands and acts which played in the festival, I saw Chuck Berry, Canned Heat, Country Joe and the Fish, Fleetwood Mac, Grateful Dead, Richie Havens, Joni Mitchell, Procol Harum, Buffy St. Marie, Steppenwolf and Three Dog Night. Most of these musicians were cast as superheroes in a commemorative comic book distributed at the event, which featured notable moments, including different acts on stage together. One example was Joni Mitchell performing with her new love interest, Graham Nash. At the time, he was a member of The Hollies but was on the cusp of beginning to work with David Crosby and Stephen Stills.

Upon my arrival, the venue's parking lot swarmed with decorated cars and vans, from which poured hordes of energized hippies. In my robust enthusiasm to attend the music festival, I did not have a ticket or money. The admission price posted on the ticket booth was $5.00. This was a significant fly in the so-called ointment since, after breakfast, there was a lonely $1.00 in my pocket.

However, I was lost in the magnitude of this monstrous event as thousands of ticket holders streamed past me toward the well-secured entry gates. My hastily improvised idea was to hear the music from the fence at the edge of the racetrack.

The event was well-fortified by a ten-foot high chain-linked fence topped with barbed wire. This barrier to potential infiltrators extended for hundreds of yards protecting this mini Fort Knox of festivals. Every few minutes, security guards patrolled the perimeter in electric golf carts searching for gate-crashers. Beyond the perimeter, additional guards on foot surveyed the scene. The last shred of hope to enter the event was dashed as I shuffled along the dusty rock-strewn pavement next to the fence. This area of the venue was quiet, unlike the frenetic atmosphere of the main entrance.

My assumption of being able to see and listen to the bands from the rear of the racetrack was mistaken. The view was obstructed by maintenance buildings, and the distance from the stage made it impossible to view or hear. My prospects dimmed as I trod the perimeter, looking for a weak link in this fortress.

I stumbled upon a rear entryway to the racetrack and, to my astonishment, it was not deserted. A sleek black limousine stopped for security. Hallelujah, here was the band entrance! I surmised the bands were being chauffeured to the venue from their hotels, and the thrill of being potentially close to some of my heroes was mind-blowing. The magnitude of this event was perfectly clear and standing outside was out of the question. I was now more determined than ever to gain entry.

The hundred-yard dash in front of me, along with several ten-foot high fences to scale, meant a forcible entry would end disastrously with either jail time or worse. Inspired by my new discovery, I plodded onward when another shiny, black limousine stopped for security next to me.

As the driver handed his pass to the security guard, I glanced at the rear side of the car, eyeing the darkly tinted window. I tapped on the glass, and it was lowered as a guy, perhaps a little older than me, peered out.

"Any chance of a ride into the festival?" I whispered eagerly.

"Get in," he answered, and the heavy door swung open. No further persuasion was necessary. My limo to the Promised Land had arrived.

I leapt in and perched on the jump seat in front of three long-haired guys on the rear bench seat. We stared at each other in silence until I asked, "Are you guys in a band?" They smiled mysteriously without responding.

"Neat trick," said the muscular one on the right.

I simply grinned as I digested my good luck.

"You come far?" the middle one asked.

"I hitched from the Keys yesterday, but I'm from Maryland," I replied.

"Yeah! Me too!" he concurred.

There wasn't time for further conversation as the limo parked in a small lot behind a single-story building. The driver opened the door, and my new rock star pals soon vanished to their dressing and rehearsal rooms.

"Enjoy the show," said the one from Baltimore, marking my initial free entry to my first pop festival. I missed their performance, no doubt I was at the other stage, but whoever they were, they saved the day. A gate-crasher was in the process of being born.

The 100,000 people in attendance danced and partied for the next three days. The relatively unknown bands performing became a part of music history, elevating their status from the opening chord. These obscure musicians, like the ones who drove me into the festival, became new superstars among the existing ones, and awesome memories were created. Steppenwolf established such a memory some six months before *Easy Rider* appeared in cinemas.

In the audience close to the stage, I chatted with several girls from Atlanta between sets when a motorcycle policeman wearing a helmet appeared. The startled audience booed, believing he planned to end the performance. He strutted across the stage and fiddled with an amp for a few moments before he spoke into the microphone.

"Greetings from the Los Angeles Police Department," said John Kay, the lead singer of Steppenwolf, as he removed his helmet.

The other band members followed onto the stage, dressed in costume; one wore a graduation cap and gown. They performed most of their first album, including *Born to Be Wild* and *The Pusher*. As they played their last song, *The Ostrich*, Kay introduced it by explaining how this song epitomized the festival. In Kay's interview for the comic book, he said the band members' costumes each symbolized the young Americans' rebellion at the time … refusing to stick their heads in the sand.

Kay's sentiment aside, I busily ran from stage to stage to hear as many bands as possible. The party atmosphere flowed after the performances ended, with festival-goers dancing, singing, drinking, and smoking all night at a local park. It was here I slept for a few hours during the next two nights.

Each morning, the parade of hippies stretched for miles as everyone marched back to the festival grounds. On the last morning, bleary eyed, I met a most enthusiastic guy. He proudly described his luck the previous night when he encountered a girl with an unusual predicament.

The young girl explained she had a limit to how many boys she screwed, never more than fifty, in one night. Once, she accidentally exceeded fifty and experienced pain and uncontrollable muscle spasms the next day. She swore to only sleep with fifty in one night. She asked my new friend to collect one dollar from every boy who went into her tent, up to fifty.

"That's what I did all night. I made fifty dollars, man!" my new friend said.

You could say this woman knew her limitations, and for a side story, fast forward six months later to Georgetown, Washington, DC. My wild and crazy friend Kurt was performing back flips on the sidewalk for 25 cents. A young girl paid to see his brief acrobatics. Moments later, she accompanied my six friends to Kurt's apartment. Her explanation was the same I heard in Miami—her limit was a maximum of fifty times in one night. I declined and went home, but my friends were happy to accommodate.

Those few days in Miami were my initiation into the new counterculture movement. The festival ended at 11:00 p.m. on December 30th and I was homeward bound. I hitchhiked on I-95 north with 25 cents in my pocket. There were few cars traveling at midnight. The situation was exacerbated by poor planning on my part because I was barely visible on the shoulder of the highway. My amateurish stab to hitchhike at midnight verged on complete foolishness as cars sailed by every two or three minutes without stopping.

At this rate, the prospect of a ride was dismal with a greater probability of arrest. The average number of cars before a ride is often in the hundreds. I repeated the hitchhiker's mantra, "The next car will stop. The next car will stop, and I will beat the odds." I was wrong. The next van stopped.

The two guys in the van introduced themselves as Steve and Harry. They almost missed me until they saw the reflection of my eyes in their headlights. Traveling to Jacksonville, Florida from the music festival, we discussed the events of the last three days before shifting to their religious beliefs.

I was confused, unfamiliar with the religious sect they referred to. Harry suggested I read their spiritual tenets, and I reluctantly agreed. He said their signed manifesto outlined their newly-formed beliefs.

The ornately decorated typewritten document, which they had both signed with a flourish, detailed their doctrine which involved Satan and human sacrifice. I read every word of the document to conceal my panic. I was uncertain if Harry was serious or joking. Would I become breakfast for an alligator somewhere in the Everglades?

According to the manifesto, in a nutshell, Harry was not joking. He effusively expounded their zeal for their new philosophy and belief in the powers of human sacrifice. Then Steve added, with equal jubilation, his belief in Satan. This was a most peculiar situation, being the first time I met two satanic worshipers.

Perhaps my haste to leave Florida was a mistake and my good luck had ended on the last note of the festival. The bizarre beliefs of these two made me extremely nervous. I frantically planned an exit strategy, but the van was speeding along I-95. Steve and Harry were anxious to hear my response. I appeared nonchalant and unperturbed. I feigned exhaustion from the festival and responded they would have my answer in the morning.

Despite the fear for my life, I was asleep in moments and did not, as expected, dream of lying on some cold stone slab as masked dancers chanted their ritual songs with death moments away. I was ecstatic to be alive the next morning as sunshine poured through the windows. I suspect one too many Alfred Hitchcock movies fueled my hyperactive imagination the previous night.

After I groggily bade them "Good morning," Harry mentioned exiting the interstate for breakfast, and my sigh of relief was short-lived. Steve swerved to exit, and the empty fields and farms rekindled my fear; I was glad it wasn't a cannibal manifesto. After a few minutes in this desolate location, a diner appeared on the horizon, and I breathed another sigh of relief.

Steve and Harry ordered fried eggs, bacon, toast, grits, and coffee. Their food was served, and I watched them eat since my 25 cents in 1968 was the same as today and afforded little. They questioned my reason for not ordering, and I was admonished for neglecting to mention my lack of money. Harry immediately offered to pay for my breakfast.

My hunger was satisfied for now. Our informal conversation at breakfast revealed the personalities of Steve and Harry to be completely at odds with their unorthodox manifesto. I shared a lively meal with two big hearted individuals who were lost and searching for answers.

Our ride resumed on I-95 heading north, and in a few hours, we were within miles of Jacksonville, their intended destination. Out of the blue, Harry became quite animated.

"Are you headed to Maryland?" he asked.

"Yes," I answered, curious where his question was leading.

"Pull alongside that car!" he instructed Steve, pointing anxiously out the window. "The one with Maryland license plates!"

Harry lowered the passenger door window and yelled at the other driver, half hanging out of the van, waving his arms, and shouting,

"Where are you going, man? Going to Maryland?"

The driver lowered his car window and answered he was headed to Baltimore. Further high-speed conversation ensued, and the guy agreed to stop. Steve pulled over on the shoulder, and I left with the Maryland driver. With a cheery wave, Steve and Harry drove away. They were the most colorful couple of guys. Being New Year's Eve, the words of *Auld Lang Syne* came to mind.

The ride with the next driver, James, was quiet in comparison. He worked in Baltimore as an office clerk and was driving home after visiting his parents in Florida for the holidays. After being dropped off, luck ruled the day with only two rides to reach within five miles of home. One more ride to reach my apartment.

I lie on my bed and listen to Steppenwolf singing The Ostrich, and now I understand John Kay's message. The drive to avoid being tied down and there being more to life than money. Our protest is that the infrastructure of the country is a mess and greed is to blame, stripping us of the Earth's natural beauty.

We detest the apathy people feel, believing they're powerless to make a change, simply hoping things will work out. We, of my generation, choose not to be the ostrich. We're free to speak our minds and believe we can shape our own

destiny ... this is what I will do as Bob Dylan sings in The Times They Are A-Changin'.

There is much good fortune to be coming of age during this period, one of the richest musical epochs-The Grateful Dead, the Beatles, Bob Dylan, Janis Joplin, Frank Zappa. The sixties are witnessing an unparalleled burst of musical creativity, ranging from Cream to Creedence Clearwater Revival to Jimi Hendrix and Neil Young to Paul Simon to Joni Mitchell.

Music of the 1960s is the voice of my generation, characteristic of the revolution. The counterculture which questions the authority of corporations, the government, and other institutions of everyday life. It is essentially a revolution to reform the status quo.

The social influences impact what popular music is and give birth to the diversity we experience today. The assassination of President Kennedy, the escalation of the war in Vietnam and the progress of the Civil Rights movement all greatly affect the mood of American culture and the music I love- and many of those in Miami-reflects that change.

As the war in Vietnam escalates, there is more music protesting the war and injustice, and for brotherhood. As the sexual revolution and drug culture progress, the songs mirror the evolution, and parents tell their children not to listen to certain songs because they might be about drugs ... if the parents don't understand the lyrics. The hippie movement echoes the changes in attitudes in the teen and young adult culture which, in turn, is heard in the music. All in all, I am glad to be a part of it.

TRACK FIVE

THE KINKS: TILL THE END OF THE DAY

1969 started with giving peace a chance. On January 3rd, the cover of John Lennon's *Two Virgins* album was deemed pornographic by the New Jersey authorities, and on January 5th, Creedence Clearwater Revival released their second album *Bayou Country*, featuring the now classic rock song *Proud Mary*. In our memories, we perhaps consider Led Zeppelin and Cream as being from the same era, but January 12th marked the former's debut album release in the U.S. and on January 23rd, the latter released their last album *Goodbye*.

On January 10th, Sweden was the first Western country to recognize North Vietnam and on January 18th, expanded four-party Vietnam peace talks, which included the United States, began in Paris. In other world news, on January 24th, Spanish dictator General Franco declared a special state of emergency, and in Bowie, MD, on this day, my life irreparably changed.

As a teenager in Bowie, the criteria for a celebration were quite low. The disappearance of a pimple, new shoes, a different hairstyle, and rain were adequate reasons. What amounted to a celebration was also simple, consisting of small talk, laughing, and smoking pot at a friend's house or driving in my beloved car or perhaps listening to tapes on my eight-track stereo system. The beginning of collegiate life was my first dip into the swimming pool of independence.

Life was good in my well-furnished bachelor pad—black light, lava lamps, a hi-fi stereo system, and eclectic posters of W.C. Fields, Albert Einstein, and a world map. My college deferment was submitted, and I hoped to avoid the draft until the Vietnam War was over. I was on track towards fulfilling my dreams of Wall Street and beyond.

Luck was on my side when I learned of the postponement in resolving my draft deferment. This related to all the records belonging to my draft board—#13—being frozen as evidence in a court case which involved the anti-war priest Philip Berrigan and several others known as 'The Baltimore Four'. Their case was extremely unusual.

As civil rights activity fomented, Berrigan and three others—artist Tom Lewis, writer David Eberhardt, and the Rev. James L. Mengel III—took radical action to highlight the anti-war movement. On October 27th, 1967, the group occupied the Selective Service Board in the Customs House in Baltimore and performed a sacrificial, blood-pouring protest, using their own blood and from pigs purchased from the Gay St. Market. They rushed through the doors and poured the blood all over the draft board files, including mine.

The trial of these individuals was postponed due to the assassination of Martin Luther King, Jr. in April '68, and the subsequent race and anti-war riots in Baltimore and other U.S. cities further extended the draft board's huge backlog. This case of the Baltimore Four proved most fortuitous for me, and thirteen became my lucky number.

In the eventual trial, Mengel stated U.S. military forces killed and maimed humans, animals, and vegetation. He refused to pour blood. Instead, he distributed the paperback book *Good News for Modern Man* (a version of the *New Testament*) to draft board workers, newsmen, and police. In his statement, Berrigan noted: "This sacrificial and constructive act" was meant to protest "the pitiful waste of American and Vietnamese blood in Indochina." Eberhardt and Lewis served jail time, and Berrigan was sentenced to six years in federal prison. The draft records were frozen in evidence for months and were not used to select men for the U.S. military.

For me, this was still the land of opportunity. The wanderlust waned as traditional aspirations awoke. The usual suspects of parents, relatives, friends, and teachers advised me to pursue an education, career, wife, children, house, etc. I was becoming convinced of the merits of working towards these more conventional goals—until tragedy forced an irrevocable U-turn.

The usual Sunday afternoon pastime of reclining on the couch listening to music was a welcome respite from the week's studies, and I looked forward to a rare quiet evening when Ernie called.

"We're going to a party tonight!" he stated cheerfully.

"Really? I was going to—"

"Oh, come on Ron! There's several happening tonight, and one is at Susie's place ..."

This was a girl I was infatuated with, and we arranged to meet at 7:45 p.m. As I drove away in my trusty Mustang, my hand delving into the bin of eight-track tapes, retrieving The Doors' debut album, a classic and personal favorite. The Mustang was trucking towards Ernie's house as the first song *Break on Through (To the Other Side)'* filled the night.

Ernie and I were friends from high school, and his qualities were numerous. The traits his friends most admired were his affability and sense of humor. He was an engaging conversationalist and was often the life of the party. After the drive from Baltimore in my brand-new car, it was heartwarming to be with my old friend.

Once settled in the passenger seat, Ernie requested listening to a tape by a band called *Spirit*. We were soon headed to the first Sunday night party, which was hosted by bartenders and servers, generally a wild and fun bunch. Pretty girls and new friends awaited at the party beyond our neighborhood. A fitting conclusion to a fun weekend; the prior Friday and Saturday nights, we were at several popular nightclubs in Washington, DC.

Ernie and I cruised down the highway, and I glanced at my watch; it was 7:59 p.m. There was a moderate amount of traffic for a Sunday night, flowing at 5 mph over the 60-mph speed limit. The *Spirit* tape played a song *Fresh Garbage*, written by singer Jay Ferguson.

I daydreamed of carousing with pretty girls at the party when I noticed a 1962 Ford Fairlane white station wagon with faux wood paneling adjacent to my car. The driver was a bald, forty-something guy, alone in his car in the passing lane. I merrily traveled in the right-hand lane and then, as though time had stopped, the maniac deliberately drove into my vehicle.

My car veered off the highway, zoomed up a four-foot embankment and catapulted into orbit. While airborne, I clutched the steering wheel in a death grip. The centrifugal force slowly pulled my fingers as the car spun through the air. The music stopped. Time was suspended.

It was eerily quiet as the car spiraled and my fingers slowly slid from the steering wheel. The perception of time and space was lost as I drifted into a strange, fearful, and perplexed state. The vehicle landed on its hardtop roof with a crunching thud. My door shot open from the impact, and I tumbled to the ground, battered and bruised.

We landed in an empty meadow, twenty yards from the highway, and I was startled to see a man, perhaps in his fifties, standing above me.

"Is there anyone in the car?" the stranger asked.

"Yes, my friend is in the passenger seat."

"Your friend is over there. I think he's dead," was the terse reply.

I slowly staggered to my feet. There were six cars stopped along the shoulder and people gathered around Ernie who lay, immobile, in the grass close to the road. My mouth was agape, digesting the last few minutes. A crazed stranger in a family station wagon had been intent on murder, and Ernie was his victim. My friends, in their efforts to provide an explanation, later assumed the motive was his hatred of our long hair and hippie looks.

Common at the time was a bumper sticker advocating killing Communists and now this intent seemed to include murdering hippies. Kill a hippie, go to heaven. Long hair was indeed a valid reason to attack someone—up to and including committing murder-during the period. In *The Atlantic,* photographer Joe Samberg recalled his arrival in Berkeley, California in '69, the area replacing Haight-Ashbury as the base for hippies:

> "When we pulled into Berkeley, the hippies were everywhere-standing on every corner, lining every avenue. I had never seen anything like it. People don't really understand this now, but at that time, in most of the country, you couldn't have long hair and not be in danger of being beaten up, or worse.

> In Boston, cars used to come screeching to a halt and guys would jump out and want to kill me. I'd have to run. In New York, whenever I left Greenwich Village, I was continually harassed, spit on, and shoved around. And I wasn't really a hippie, I was just 'hip' and that meant boots, black jeans, a black t-shirt, a leather jacket-the kind of thing you'd maybe see the Rolling Stones wearing."

In a stupor, I gawked at the upside-down Mustang, and its contents scattered on the ground—music tapes, car mats, maps, etc., including my shoes. I was barefoot except for my socks; the centrifugal force had yanked the shoes off my feet. The real damage was psychological. Somewhere in the dark meadow that night lay the shattered remnants of my mind.

Ernie's door was wrapped beneath the undercarriage, and based on his body's location on the ground, it was later determined he was hurled from the car on the initial spin. In disbelief, I saw his immobile body and expressionless eyes. The tragedy intensified from an atrocious nightmare to the worst kind of reality.

The police arrived on the scene to investigate. Unfortunately, none of the witnesses, including our friend Pete in the car behind us, noted the driver's license plate number. The next day, the Washington Post reported the incident, and the police stated the action of the driver was deliberate. The subsequent police investigation failed to apprehend the culprit, and the angry driver eluded justice. My wish was for his deathbed confession, but this longing has so far remained unfulfilled.

The next day, final exam week was due to commence and, once more, my world was collapsing faster than a snowman on a hot summer's day. A few days later, friends and family gathered for Ernie's funeral. It was a sunny yet gloomy day as sadness permeated the chapel. The unanswered questions after an unfathomable event loomed over everyone.

I attempted to answer Ernie's distraught parents' questions in my traumatized state, particularly why Ernie was not wearing his seat belt. They spoke of Ernie's promise to always wear one because of his previous involvement in two serious automobile accidents. This was one question I was unable to answer, and his parents recognized the anguish we all faced. They understood it was a tragedy, yet at times it was difficult not to blame myself.

In my confused state, one thing became undeniable: Pursuing a normal career would only vindicate the horrible system that led to Ernie's death. I was through with America. I didn't want it, and it didn't want me except possibly as cannon fodder. It was the worst of times, and I dropped out of college.

I equated my salvation with the open road. This led to my application for a U.S. passport, and days later, it arrived in the mail. In despair, I grasped for a life preserver and prayed travel would be the antidote.

> *Ernie is gone. CS Lewis said, "Friendship is unnecessary, like philosophy, like art ... it has no survival value; rather it is one of those things which gives value to survival." At the end of the day, friendship is deep and powerful, yet something difficult to describe. If you lose a close friend, I mourn for you and them.*

> *When a friend dies, like when a family member dies, we don't 'get over it'; we learn to live with it. Life becomes different; the love endures. Why is losing a friend particularly isolating?*

> *Cultures often value family relationships above friendships. There is a weight given to your relationship with your parents, siblings, grandparents, or spouse based on their titles. Somehow, discussing your best friend often doesn't carry the same weight; a friend dies, and you may not receive the same support and validation as a family member. However, your relationship with your friend may have been as, if not more, important.*

> *Your friend is the person who also comforted you during the ugly side of life. Life becomes turbulent and your best friend is often your go-to person—this explains my visit to Ernie the first day I bought the Mustang. The loss is devastating,*

and your instinct is to call out to the one person who is no longer there to support you.

In my living room, looking through the window across the balcony and courtyard into the trees, I pictured all the beautiful places there are in the world to visit. Somewhere, deep inside me, the idea percolated that it was time to run from the madness of conventional existence. My second attempt at developing a 'mainstream' lifestyle was doomed. Like everyone else, my ultimate desire was to find happiness. Surely this existed for me somewhere in the world.

TRACK SIX

DEEP PURPLE: BIRD HAS FLOWN

The daily news events of the intensifying Vietnam War, coupled with my urge to flee the U.S., advanced my aim of circling the world. My first foray into international travel occurred in early February '69 when I boarded a flight from New York City to Tel Aviv. A friend suggested the benefits of volunteering on a kibbutz. Kibbutz life was a logical remedy to provide natural healing somewhere far from the memories of Ernie's death.

A kibbutz, the Hebrew word for 'group', is a collective community in Israel, in which there is no private wealth, and it is responsible for all the needs of the members and their families. It encompasses the team effort between members, working and living together to achieve business goals through agriculture and manufacturing. The idea was a magnet for many backpackers from around the world, and in 1969, the kibbutz movement numbered some 93,000 people in 231 kibbutzim.

Organized according to social, political, and religious outlooks, the kibbutz provided a complete spectrum of services to its members, ranging from razor blades to housing and from honeymoons to financial aid for dependents living outside, with complete medical coverage.

The early morning routine at Kibbutz Amir, based in the upper Galilee region of northern Israel, involved harvesting grapefruit in the orchard, a slightly hazardous task since the twelve-foot tall grapefruit trees had an abundance of sharp thorns. While balanced on a ladder, I and others quickly developed a technique to carefully pick the fruit while avoiding bloody cuts from the wrist to the elbow. The simple skill involved a nimble action in snaking one's arm to follow the tree branches before promptly picking the fruit.

The process of picking grapefruit consists of two parts—collecting from the ground and via a ladder. For either part of the tree, the grapefruits were placed in a cross-body sack holding approximately forty grapefruits which were carefully emptied into a crate. It was obvious to spot novice grapefruit pickers by the cuts on their arms, but harvesting these aggressive trees was preferable to working in the chicken house or gathering cotton, other options for kibbutz volunteers.

One morning, Horatio, a fellow American traveler, and I consumed a hearty breakfast in the dining hall after work in the orchard. Usually talkative, on this day he was in deep thought, and I inquired why. Horatio described he was lost in the 'stay or go' syndrome. He was in search of his true self, and the kibbutz offered only a temporary slice of paradise. Still seeking to escape the grasp of his domineering mother, Horatio finally opted to fly to Mykonos, Greece the following week. Paradise lasts until something better arises, I concluded.

The wide range of nationalities among the volunteers added a mix of cultural differences to appreciate. A variety of perspectives of the world converged among the flamboyant cast of characters. The new surroundings, friends, and work helped provide everyone with distractions. Some merely perceived the kibbutz as a chance to visit a new and different country; however, there were many, like Horatio and I, who had other, deeper reasons.

The living arrangements consisted of rows of barracks-style accommodations, with each 'block' having six individual furnished bedrooms and three common bathrooms. I shared a bedroom with

Anton, a Czech fellow who fled his country in the aftermath of the Soviet invasion during the 'Prague Spring' of the previous year. All of us slept on comfortable straw mattresses, and incidentals were provided. Although we were volunteers, we were paid ten dollars per month.

The swimming pool was a popular gathering place in the warmer months. My refuge on sleepless nights was the deserted swimming pool when it was empty during the cooler months.

An empty, drained swimming pool is an excellent location for meditation. The moon shines brightly as I descend to the bottom of the pool and recline by the wall. My eyes closed, I picture the moon with a huge smile directed at me. I smile at the moon.

What is it all about? My questions are numerous, yet the answers I have are confusing. A different hairstyle leads to murder? A death sentence from a judgmental person whose primary intent is to kill.

A random event led to the formation of a new plan of action for my life. The traditional path disintegrated twice, and the best goal is no plan at all. I will allow serendipity to chart my course in life. The sense of control and stability was fleeting. The plan of no plan suits someone who sits in an empty pool when everyone is asleep.

The turmoil of this decade is firing wildly, affecting thousands of people in diverse ways. I consider my own situation. I blame my red hair for being a magnet to attract insane people. In class, a teacher accused me of being disruptive. I was innocent, yet immediately pinned with the blame. Upon reflection, this analogy made perfect sense. I was the first person seen by the Fairlane driver. Where in the lottery of life will the fickle finger point next?

Despite my adjustment to kibbutz life, not every day was filled with conversation and laughter. I was confused and lost, often blind to the growing inner turmoil. I paid the price for the abuse I suffered at home which resulted in panic attacks. There were various random triggers, for example, running faucet water, certain smells, sounds, and visual cues precipitating flashbacks. Generally, the episodes may last days before subsiding, and the first hours are the worst. I use the present tense because they recur to this day.

The most frequent type of attack is anxiety-driven fear. These attacks are sometimes compounded with severe stomach pains, fainting spells, and anxiety-driven sleep. Today, my diagnosis is PTSD. The symptoms today are identical to the ones I experienced as a child, and the traumatic events which occurred later in my life—Ernie's death for example—only exacerbated the problem. This unsettling mood was amplified when my draft notice to be inducted into the U.S. Army arrived in April '69. Once the court released the draft board records, the draft board expediently resumed their work.

My timing to leave the U.S. was the correct decision. A month after I dropped out of school, my prior college deferment was reclassified to 1A. I was eligible to be drafted into the U.S. Army. In a letter from my mother, she had notified the draft board of my absence from the country. The clerk said they would call me upon my return from Europe. It was a relief my draft board was in favor of my travels, although I could not escape the net cast by the U.S. Army. It was a distressing decision to return home to resolve my draft notice.

The Battle of Hamburger Hill commenced on May 10th, 1969 and raged in Vietnam. The heavily fortified Hill 937 was of little strategic value, but U.S. command ordered its capture by direct assault. American soldiers there dubbed it 'Hamburger Hill' suggesting those who fought on the hill were "chewed up like a hamburger". It was a grim reference to the Battle of Pork Chop Hill during the Korean War.

It was not an appetizing picture to be the next slice of beef as I flew home on May 12th to proactively comply with my draft notice. Thanks to the Baltimore Four, the draft board was preoccupied for now. There was no rush to contact the draft board until I had a method to avoid my induction into the U.S. Army. In my bedroom in Bowie, lost in a fog, I stuffed their letter in the desk drawer. Now what? As a distraction, I thumbed the pages of a week-old Washington Post, and a half-page advertisement for an airfare sale to Jamaica caught my attention.

The sale was a round trip from Miami to Jamaica. After a few phone calls, two friends were on board. One was 'backflip' Kurt and the other was Roger, who provided transportation to Miami. Kurt was an experienced backpacker, eager to smoke pot in Jamaica or anywhere else. Roger, recently separated from his wife, was also ready for an escape.

We departed Bowie in Roger's VW convertible for the first leg of our journey, a twenty-four-hour ride to Miami. The billboards along Interstate 95 advertised Pedro waiting for us 150 miles away at the South of the Border attraction, which included a restaurant and souvenir shops. Well, it was 150 miles at first, and every five or ten miles there was another billboard with a reminder stating how excited Pedro was for our arrival. Pedro was enthusiastic for our visit. "Si," said Pedro.

Kurt's turn to drive began at midnight. Roger and I rested before our next shift. I fell asleep in the front passenger seat, as did Roger in the back seat. In my sleepy delirium, a hand tapped my shoulder, and Kurt calmly asked me to wake up.

"Huh?" I replied groggily.

"You should drive," he informed me.

"OK, where are we?"

"I fell asleep, and we're in a cornfield somewhere in Georgia," answered Kurt.

"Holy crap!" was my response as I was suddenly wide awake.

Another dance with the Grim Reaper sent my adrenaline into hyperspace. I blinked a few times and saw the dark outline of corn stalks surrounding the car. The highway was 100 yards behind us. This was a strange and disturbing awakening.

Now in the driver's seat, I mulled over the fact that all three of us had slept through a brush with mortality. Obscure happenings at night are not unknown and waking up dead is not an ideal way to start the day. Well, there is no reason to dwell, but I am here, and not in the netherworld playing poker with James Dean. I assumed the farmer was not upset with our nocturnal escapade.

The remainder of the trip was mundane and uneventful. We arrived in downtown Kingston at 8:00 p.m. Ready to enjoy our first evening on Jamaican soil, this was our mistake, as we were white rice on asphalt in a seedy neighborhood. The realization dawned that this was the wrong place at the wrong time as large rocks rained all around us. This was not the welcome we expected, and it explained the airfare sale on Air Jamaica. We panicked and ran for our lives.

Since 1962, there were important developments in infrastructure and education in Jamaica, and their cultural heritage was heavily promoted. Investments in tourism, bauxite, and capital-intensive light manufacturing industries fueled economic growth. However, the expanding economy failed to absorb the growing workforce which led to unrest.

The bulldozing of squatter communities in West Kingston and the recruitment by both political parties of elements (including criminal ones) of the inner city to fight their political wars increased disaffection and violence in urban communities. In 1967, the government imposed a state of emergency in West Kingston, and while things calmed down, it was still a volatile place.

Fortunately, the three of us ran toward a bus that had stopped, and we frantically jumped aboard. I asked the bus driver if he was leaving Kingston. He nodded and said he was going to Bull Bay. I paid the fare, happy to escape with our lives unscathed despite the fact we were clueless about Bull Bay which was as dark as a movie theater when we arrived.

Upon exiting the bus, we bumped into each other until a young man appeared out of the gloom and offered to be our guide. Introducing himself as Oscar, he was friendlier than his Kingston counterparts, and we followed him through the neighborhood to his parents' shack. We became the main tourist attraction; at least there was a welcome reception this time. Oscar confirmed Kingston was unsafe day and night.

We congregated around the roaring campfire in front of the shack with other residents. We were thankful to unwind after our rocky arrival in Kingston as Oscar made introductions. Oscar's father Bob was the unofficial leader of this small village, and he welcomed us. The Three Stooges of Bull Bay, as we dubbed ourselves, were the evening's entertainment.

All the locals around the campfire were interested in life in the U.S. compared to Jamaica. Surrounded by tin shacks, it was foreign for the residents of Bull Bay to comprehend the "lavish" middle-class lifestyle in the U.S. Bob shared some ganja (Jamaican pot). As we smoked a gigantic spliff, the now overly animated group talked into the night. Blissfully, we passed out around the campfire as the weary travelers fell into a deep sleep.

I was the last one to awake the next day, and the news was Kurt ran off with a two-dollar hooker. Apparently, they were getting it on somewhere in the surf. Someone stole Roger's pants and shirt from his pack, and my eyeglasses were also missing. I alerted Bob who said, "I'll take care of it." He was true to his word, and within fifteen minutes, all the missing items reappeared.

When Kurt returned with his lust duly sated, Bob advised it was unsafe for us to remain in Bull Bay. He suggested riding the bus to Ocho Rios, a tourist town fifty-miles away. We thanked Bob and Oscar for their hospitality and left a few dollars.

Traveling along the coast road, the bus to Ocho Rios also served as the means to transport commerce. Many passengers boarded with live chickens, eggs, and other assorted farm products. Every small town we passed through had an open-air café with a jukebox where people gathered and listened to Bob Marley's latest hits as our former fellow passengers sought to sell their wares to the proprietors.

It was a hot, humid Jamaica day upon our arrival in Ocho Rios along the north coast road. Exhausted from the six-hour bus ride, we wandered aimlessly in the ninety plus degree heat, both hungry and dehydrated. We collapsed, drenched in perspiration on the ground near the road. I inhaled deeply and relaxed as the long palm fronds above provided shade. I fell asleep.

Before long, a jolly rotund man with a wide, toothy smile ambled over. "I noticed you from my café, and you are welcome to visit," he said with a smile, but I politely declined his offer. Kurt and Roger were penniless, and I was now the sole provider. I thanked the kind café owner and explained we were poor backpackers. This was not an obstacle, according to this charming and ebullient fellow.

"No problem, man. I love Americans coming to my café. You can eat and drink for free. Don't worry about paying because I will charge the next group of Americans double to cover the cost of your food!"

We accepted the magnanimous offer, and I imagined the next set of Americans were generous. We were rejuvenated by our free food and drink, a happy contrast to our stony welcome. This was the Jamaica of my dreams. Reinvigorated, off we went down the road to scout a suitable location to camp for the evening. We were fortunate to soon stumble upon a lovely white sandy beach with a quiet cove and the bluest of waters. An abandoned beach cabana was a major bonus.

This was a magical place, with a stunning view of the sea framed by gently swaying coconut trees. This was five-star camping, and much more than we expected. We unrolled our sleeping bags to lie down and relax, inhaling the fresh sea air before we cast off our clothes and dove into the warm sea. This was heavenly, and before long, it was the trio of beach bums who were the star attraction.

A group of five kids aged eight to fourteen breezed in as the oldest and tallest introduced himself as Pepsi. My burning question was the origin of his name, and he eagerly provided the explanation.

"Mon, there was a large billboard next to our house, and when I was born, my mother screamed "Pepsi is the best!" as she read the billboard advertising Pepsi-Cola. My mother proclaimed what better name for her son!"

Now it all made sense.

Pepsi explained his offer to help us and, as promised, he and his friends arrived on schedule the next morning with food, ganja, and handmade spear guns.

"There's a river 'bout 500 yards from here. It's perfect for swimming and diving and we'll spear fish for lunch," Pepsi suggested. We devoured a traditional breakfast of ackee, the national fruit of Jamaica, and salt fish.

Roger, Kurt, and I trotted to the river with our newfound friends who led us to a well-hidden location surrounded by trees. We were astonished this oasis was nearby. On one side was a sheer rock face rising fifty feet above the twenty-foot deep crystal-clear river. It was an idyllic location, and we never guessed this existed next to our campsite. We tried our best at spear fishing without success, and Pepsi, the expert fisherman, caught lunch for us while we swam above.

We were putting on the Ritz with fresh fish, coconuts, bread, vegetables, and ganja at our campsite, and this became our daily routine for five days. As we toured our neighborhood down the road for a change of scenery, we concluded our campsite was in the best location.

While misfortune was the order of the day in Kingston, the opposite was the case here. Or so we thought. Upon our return to the campsite, we were alarmed to observe two heavyset men rifling through our backpacks. We sprinted to confront them.

"Hello," I said, "these are our backpacks and sleeping bags."

The two men stood their ground.

"Who are you?" one asked.

"We're Americans," I answered.

Now their whole demeanor changed, and they smiled with relief. The taller man introduced himself as Tom. He owned the land, and his fear was we were Cuban refugees. Now gracious and friendly, he described his plans to build a luxury hotel where we camped, but until then, we were welcome to stay. I now presume there is an upscale hotel because today, Ocho Rios is a top tourist destination and a port of call for cruise ships.

Our last night in Ocho Rios was cause for celebration with a night out on the town. We walked the seventy-five yards from our campsite to the road to hitch a ride. A motorist stopped and offered to drive us to town. The driver asked the name of our hotel. In hindsight, I suspected it was odd to see three guys hitchhiking in a desolate location.

"We're not staying at a hotel; we're sleeping down the road," explained Roger.

"Oh man, you're the campers!" The driver chuckled and said his name was Frank.

We were naïve to believe no one noticed us for the last five days when apparently, everyone within several miles was aware of our presence.

"This is our last night, and we're celebrating with dinner," Roger added.

"No problem, man. My cousin owns the best restaurant in the village," said Frank.

The celebrity campers were elevated to VIP status as we entered the restaurant. Frank ran into the kitchen and escorted his cousin Nelson, who was introduced to us with the type of enthusiasm usually reserved for royalty. Nelson instantly said to expect the grandest dinner ever, accompanied by free beers. Nelson was incredibly big-hearted, and we were indeed happy campers. Another shining example of the good nature of Jamaicans.

We boarded a bus in the morning traversing through the Blue Mountains of Jamaica instead of retracing the coastal route. Thus, we circumvented being stoned in Kingston a second time and reached the airport safe and sound in time for our return flight. Soon we were in the air and homeward bound to Miami.

After we landed, the drive to Bowie was initially uneventful. In Georgia at 4:00 a.m., thanks again to Kurt's creative driving, we drove on desolate country roads, when a frantic man abruptly materialized in the middle of the road. He was in distress, leaping up and down in a frenzy, waving his shirt above his head. Kurt cautiously slowed the car in case the man was a highway robber.

The half-dressed, panic-stricken man desperately begged for assistance. He was attacked by two hitchhikers, who tossed him out of his car before they drove off with his wallet and other possessions. It was a disturbing drive to the police station as he repeated his story over and over. At an all-night gas station, the attendant provided directions to the only police station in the area, and we left him in the safe hands of the authorities.

A person in distress on a dark, quiet country road is a classic scenario favored by highway robbers intent on violence. It is difficult to discern if help is legitimate. A victim fallen prey to an attack was a reversal in normal expectations. Whatever the circumstances, I witnessed the dark side of hitchhikers and the risks for drivers. The assumption is sincerity and trusting your instincts. The unfortunate outcome was irreversible damage to this man's psyche.

Our last penny was spent on gasoline, and we were lucky when the last toll collector on I-95 in Virginia waived the fee. I dozed in the back seat, and once our tank was empty, it was up to Roger or Kurt to beg for fuel. I awoke to see the stern of my father's sailboat on a trailer and read the familiar name "Maru."

"Pull alongside the driver with the boat!" I yelled to Roger.

The driver was my father transporting his sailboat from Florida to Annapolis and was astounded when he saw me gesticulating wildly out the car window yelling at him to stop. He did so, and our fuel expenses to Bowie were solved when I borrowed five dollars, plenty for gasoline in 1969 when it cost 35 cents per gallon. The outlandish exploits which occur to the wandering wayfarers are, for them, normal. This happened to me time after time. The campers see Jamaica.

"Si," said Pedro.

TRACK SEVEN

THE MOTHERS OF INVENTION: BROWN SHOES DON'T MAKE IT

Motionless from the endless drudgery of being pushed back and forth from the supermarket, like a drunken robot, a shopping cart lay on its side next to the department store wall adjacent to the parking lot. Tucked away in the shade, it beckoned the hot and weary to sit and escape the humid June heat. This was my improvised bench for my rendezvous with Kurt in the shopping plaza, our local hangout. It was peaceful and quiet, until my hair was a beacon for trouble.

This time, my antagonist was a vigilant local patrol officer whom I shall refer to as Officer H. A somewhat portly gentleman in his thirties, with the buttons on his shirt straining to escape a probable hefty lunch, his duty and obligation were to protect the shoppers. The essence of his concern was stray shopping carts should be immediately reunited with their brethren in the supermarket corral. Law and order must prevail, and no shopper should be without a cart. Within seconds, the mistake of innocence was apparent.

"I didn't bring it here," I replied when he ordered me to return the wayward cart.

"You will return the shopping cart, or I will arrest you!" he declared, hands on his hips in a gesture of self-importance.

I was not the person who abandoned or upended the poor beast, but the stray cart catcher was not in the mood for arguments or frivolity. I brought the cart to an upright position and pushed it one hundred yards to the supermarket. Officer H. closely followed to give the poor four-wheeled creature added protection. The seriousness, value, and importance of a shopping cart were to be safeguarded at all costs from the wandering butts of weary long-haired youths.

I was now acutely aware that this simple conveyance held the fabric of our society together. The shopping cart has one specific role— to transport goods for payment—case closed. The wayward cart successfully rejoined its comrades, awaiting the next customer. I waved goodbye to Officer H. as he menacingly stated, "You are under arrest."

This was a perplexing turn of events, and Officer H.'s principles were offended. I was handcuffed and escorted to the police station in his patrol car.

Required to sit in a stark interview room with the scent of a previous visitor's vomit, the nature of my shocking crime was revealed: I disrupted a female customer's shopping experience. Officer H. explained the woman exited Marty's Cards gift shop and was *forced* to wait until I pushed the shopping cart beyond the door. Long-haired youths *must* conform to good manners … or else.

This bizarre experience was not an isolated incident during this period in America. Other friends were arrested for similarly petty if not wholly invented offenses. The well-orchestrated campaign by federal, state, and county authorities versus the dreaded long-haired hippies was at its peak. The traditionalists were in full force to maintain the so-called 'status quo' in the U.S.

I paid a one-hundred-dollar bond to avoid jail until the court date, which was scheduled in thirty days. A haircut was the rule of the day to dodge sixty days in jail plus a haircut. In other words, a haircut before the court case ensured the usual sentence of probation. Whereas if you didn't cut your hair first before court, jail time was guaranteed, and the jail's barber administered a crew cut with a buzz razor. One of my friends said it seemed an expedient scheme to persuade teenagers to abide by the rules of society. Others also considered it sound advice to shear my locks to avoid jail.

I debated the pros and cons of the loss of my flowing locks versus my alleged crime and the entire judicial process. In reference to our country, the mood at the time was "Love it or leave it". "Kill the Communists" and "Burn yourself, not the flag" are self-explanatory. For some reason, these sentiments related to anyone with long hair. We were, at the least, equal to Communists if not lower on the totem pole. "Beware of long-haired hippies," was broadcast on the evening news, amassing unintended support for the counterculture movement.

More and more young men adopted a long-haired hippie style when the simple fact was the ruling class only accepted long hair on women. It wasn't obvious why there was a high price to pay for sporting long hair.

On my day in court, I opted to face my charge of causing a public nuisance without a haircut. In preparation for court, I formulated my defense strategy. After all, the stigma of becoming the man who failed to push a shopping cart properly was at stake.

In the bathroom mirror, the reflection of my long red hair shone brighter than a matador's cape. The stage was set to step into the ring with a bull called Officer H. as the judge offered either the sword or the scissors—the choice to slay myself or cut my hair. Samson's dilemma.

I opened the medicine cabinet to retrieve my toothbrush and toothpaste. In a trance, I brushed my teeth and peered at the top shelf of the cabinet. Voila! There was the answer to the problem! A lone roll of gauze bandage was the solution. I will cut my hair without cutting my hair. With teeth gleaming in the mirror, I merrily bandaged my head until only my face was exposed. I was transformed into a wounded warrior.

I was nervous as hell in the courtroom gallery awaiting my case. Silently, I practiced how to express my case clearly and concisely to the judge. I intended to plead my case without a lawyer under the assumption the truth would prove my innocence. The advice of an attorney was to accept a plea deal; I had a better idea.

My case was called, and I sat alone at the defendant's table. On the opposite side of the aisle, the prosecution team, comprised of the district attorney, assistant district attorney, and Officer H., was assembled. On the hard, wooden chair, with a deep breath, I hoped the scales of justice were fair.

The district attorney questioned Officer H., seeking his detailed description of the wanton pushing of a shopping cart by said defendant, and the near collision between a shopper and the cart. I developed my defense from what was not said. Officer H. emphasized the poor female shopper's delay as she exited the supermarket. The district attorney rested his case with a smug grin, and the judge asked if I had questions for the witness.

"Yes, Your Honor, I do have questions," I confidently answered as I rose to my feet and walked towards Officer H.

"Under the threat of arrest, did you force the defendant to return the cart to the Food Fair supermarket?" I questioned.

He hesitated before responding in the affirmative.

"Was anyone injured during the shopping cart's return?"

"No."

"Did you supervise the defendant and the cart?"

"Well, I ..."

"Answer the question please," interjected the judge who realized Officer H. and the DA were wasting his time.

"Yes," he replied, anticipating what was coming next. I had one more question.

"As an officer of the law, is it your responsibility to protect citizens?"

"Yes."

"I have no further questions, Your Honor." I rested my case and returned to my lonely table.

The judge flashed Officer H. a stern look and rendered his verdict.

"I do not condone what you did, and I find the defendant not guilty," he bellowed as he banged his gavel with finality.

Although the overt reason given by the prosecution was that I had endangered a female with a shopping cart, one I had been forced to move under the watchful supervision of Officer H., it was obvious the reason I was targeted was because of my long hair. The following day, one of my friends who was in the courtroom during the case, described what he overheard between the bailiff and Officer H. The bailiff inquired if I was beaten by Officer H. who said he expected me to receive sixty days in jail, "with or without a haircut."

His view on my punishment also included banishment from the shopping center forever.

I was banned from the Belair Shopping Center, the local gathering place for the area's teenagers, effective immediately. I was prohibited from entering both the shopping center and parking lot. Who issued the ban? Officer H.! In my opinion, Officer H. overstepped his authority, but I was not overly perturbed. My friends and I agreed the corner of my street was the new hangout. A convenient and popular meeting place was born, free from shopping carts and overbearing patrol officers with fat stomachs.

My draft problem remained unresolved at the time, but there were attempts to take action on the war. President Richard Nixon and South Vietnamese President Nguyễn Văn Thiệu met at Midway Island and, as a result, Nixon ordered the withdrawal of 25,000 U.S. troops by September '69. The first of these occurred on July 8th.

On June 22nd, The National Convention of the Students for a Democratic Society (SDS), held in Chicago, collapsed as the faction known colloquially as the Weathermen seized control of the SDS National Office. The Weathermen's primary goal was to create a clandestine revolutionary party to overthrow the U.S. Government. Six days later, the Stonewall riots in New York City marked the start of the modern gay rights movement in the U.S.

After my day in court, in contrast, my life was less chaotic. My efforts to resolve my draft problem were stressful, but I studiously followed my plan to have no plan. I initially declined my friends' suggestion to attend the Laurel Pop Festival, to be held on June 11th and 12th, ten miles from my house. They requested my prowess in gaining free entry. I then received persuasive news which changed my mind.

Until the last minute, I was unaware of the full details of the band line-up for the two days, having only heard snippets of the schedule on the radio. Then my friend nicknamed Tulip rushed in breathlessly at lunchtime the day before.

"Ron, you must go to the festival!" she gasped, standing in my kitchen.

"Why?" I queried.

"Because Frank Zappa's playing!"

That was it. One of my favorite bands was The Mothers of Invention, led by Frank Zappa, and now I was immediately sold on the idea. Tickets were ten dollars, and after my prior successes, I was determined to gain free entry. I mulled ideas that afternoon to no avail until I changed clothes for an evening out; the solution hung in the closet.

From my time as a mailman, the postal service uniform hung in my closet and now was the time for its resurrection. On the first day of the festival, I donned the gray uniform. Now I needed a prop. The hippie mailman needed something to deliver. I rifled through the desk drawers for an envelope to complete my persona. The envelope was a little creased, but I flattened it out and wrote the address:

Special Delivery!

Mr. Frank Zappa
Laurel Pop Festival
Laurel, MD

A piece of paper was nowhere to be found, and in its absence, I frantically thrust a People's Drug Store receipt in the envelope and sealed it. In my haste to leave, I neglected to complete the return address or place a stamp on the envelope. I was on a mission to see Frank Zappa.

My stroke of genius was to enter through the press gate. This was the best option because of lesser security versus the main gate. I marched boldly through the front door marked 'Press Only' with my envelope held high above my head shouting, "Special Delivery for Frank Zappa! Letter for Frank Zappa! I must get in right away!" My billowing long red hair and my official postal service hat were incongruous for the time. My ruse did not fool the seated security official.

A lengthy line of reporters stood in line on the far side of the room and, by default, I was the pre-show entertainment. The dubious security guy requested the envelope, which I handed to him. He suspiciously commented, "There isn't a stamp on the envelope." I reiterated, "Special Delivery for Frank Zappa, I must enter, sir!"

In the background, several sympathetic reporters hollered, "Let him in!" They were not deceived by my disguise but believed my effort was worthy of free entry. A soon-to-be-famous reporter from the Washington Post yelled several times in support of my entry, and the security guard was swayed in my favor.

"I can't allow you to pass through the press gate—Frank Zappa is not here until tomorrow. Go to the main entrance gate; I'm sure you'll get in," he advised as he handed the envelope back to me with a wink.

"Thanks, Officer!" I replied as I hurried outside.

For my next attempt at the main gate, I held the empty envelope aloft as I passed the turnstiles shouting, "Special Delivery for Frank Zappa! I must get in right away! Letter for Frank Zappa!" The busy ticket collectors, oblivious to the set-list on the posters behind them, barely noticed me. The over the moon hippie mailman triumphantly paraded into the festival.

Despite the delay in seeing Frank Zappa's performance, there was awesome music the first night. The evening commenced with blues guitarist Buddy Guy, followed by the Edwin Hawkins Singers, and Al Kooper, the ex-lead singer of Blood, Sweat and Tears. Next were Jethro Tull and then Johnny Winter. The night's headliners were Led Zeppelin, amid their first worldwide tour.

It was late, and after a few songs, Robert Plant's microphone was muted following complaints from nearby residents. He was irate and sang louder than the band! The microphone was briefly turned on once more, and the band played until all the power was cut off. I lost my new pair of eyeglasses in the pandemonium of the festival's first day.

"My name is Joy, and my sister is Frieda. Let's go to the Sock Hop." I will dance with Frieda and jump with Joy.

Forward over the hill to see what is on the other side. All the chicks that crossed the road before me. Do not be afraid, it is only what you see, not what will be.

I step on to the ice-covered slide in June. The ride doesn't stop until December. Where am I? Who am I? Slippery Richard speaks, "We are all zombies from your past, and you are now a stranger in a strange land." I step forward to shake Richard's hand. "It is a pleasure to meet y'all." "I am in a hurry," Richard says, "Talk to you later."

Once more resplendent in my mailman uniform, the next day I hitchhiked to the festival and hustled to the main gate. Here I repeated my performance and was as successful with the same letter, albeit now more crumpled.

The final night's line-up was equally as impressive, but the night was problematic as rain delayed the performances for two hours. The restless fans lingered in the cold downpour until finally, at 10:00 p.m., the Jeff Beck Group, with Rod Stewart and Ronnie Wood, performed on stage. The next act was Ten Years After, followed by The Guess Who and then The Mothers of Invention. Sly and the Family Stone concluded the festival and brought the house down.

In the lull before The Mothers of Invention's performance, I spotted Tulip, who, with some other friends, climbed a high fence and ran past the few security guards. To escape the rain, we slipped behind the stage and found a secluded area with trailers and catering tents. Temporarily dry beneath a tent canopy, we smoked hashish together.

"The show will resume in ten minutes!" was announced as the rain subsided.

I squinted through the haze of my intoxication, questioning my already impaired vision. There was no doubt. Frank Zappa had materialized roughly thirty yards in front of us.

"Let's go say hello to Frank," I said to Tulip, nodding in his direction.

"We can't do that, Ron!" she said, putting a restraining hand on my arm.

"Oh yes we can!" I countered, and Tulip followed. We briskly moseyed over, me resplendent in my soaked U.S. Postal Service uniform. In deference to the man and his song *Brown Shoes Don't Make It,* I wore black ones.

A song from The Mothers of Invention's second album *Absolutely Free* often known simply as *Brown Shoes* is one of Frank Zappa's most widely renowned works, declared by some as being his first real masterpiece. The title was inspired by an event covered by *Time* magazine reporter Hugh Sidey in 1966, when the usually fastidiously dressed President Lyndon B. Johnson committed the sartorial faux pas of wearing brown shoes with a gray suit.

As Frank eyed my now limp red hair under my sagging and shapeless mailman's hat, I recounted the letter ruse. I handed him the envelope and explained.

"Mr. Zappa, I used your name to enter the festival with this envelope," I recounted.

"That was a great ploy," he replied with a laugh, "and call me Frank." He was suitably impressed and grinned as he said, "We're about to go on, so be my guests and sit at the front of the stage."

The wildest fantasy imaginable came true. An outrageous foray to locate a dry place to smoke hash became the chance of a lifetime. This truly was a mind-blowing, dumb luck, outlandish happening. The soggy mailman was unexpectedly thrust into the limelight. We listened incredulously from the front side of the stage as if this was a private performance.

On the stage, I was oblivious to the fact I was visible to the entire audience. I could not believe my good fortune to meet my favorite musician. For a moment, I was the only person at the show. I never expected to personally deliver my bogus letter to him, and now I was on stage, in the best location, to see and hear his performance. I was mesmerized for the entire duration.

The band played a characteristically absurd set, seeking to mock all things serious, and Frank Zappa's brilliance shone through. By the time his ten-man show left the stage, it was 1:00 a.m., with two remaining acts. In the cold early hours of the morning, piled into large bonfires, the audience started to burn their wooden folding chairs to keep warm.

Following a lengthy set-up time and an announcement pleading, "The management has asked you to please not burn the chairs," Sly and the Family Stone appeared on stage around 2:00 a.m. In the intervening time, as I meandered through the crowd towards the bathroom, I constantly heard whispers of, "There's the mailman!" It was odd to be recognized, and I imagined everyone believing I was Frank Zappa's latest attempt at subtle humor.

The following week after the concert, I was unsuccessful at hitchhiking to New York City. On a hot summer's day, stranded near Baltimore, I aborted the trip. Dehydrated, lying on the side of the road, another hitchhiker across the road ended his trip. He headed in my direction toward the highway exit ramp. As I gazed at him, he exclaimed, "Hey, you're the mailman!" as he strolled past.

My mailman escapade and my shopping cart caper led to my belief in seeing 'the light at the end of the tunnel'. Post-festival, I danced on a cloud of happiness in a sea of tranquility. These happy endings restored my confidence. I was now running with the lions across the savanna, but to this day, I am apprehensive to push a shopping cart. My exaggerated sense of responsibility is enormous.

TRACK EIGHT

JIMI HENDRIX:
STAR-SPANGLED BANNER

I attended many concerts in addition to music festivals, seeing nearly every major band of the late sixties and early seventies era. My expertise in gaining free entry to music events progressed, as more friends solicited my assistance. The record number of people I helped gain free admission is eight friends at once, and this was when we 'attended' the sold-out Led Zeppelin concert in the Baltimore Civic Center on July 23rd, 1973.

While some 14,500 lucky ticket holders filed inside, groups of despondent fans without a ticket circled the building, trying to open doors to no avail. Press reports the following day estimated nearly four thousand people were milling around outside the arena, desperate to purchase tickets at the last minute.

Meanwhile, I marched confidently through the press gate and presented my authentic *Orlando Sentinel* press pass, a gift from a friend. The security official scrutinized the pass and consulted a list on a clipboard. He apologetically shook his head. I was denied entry because my name was not on the approved list of reporters. I urged him to reconsider, speaking of being fired for not filing my report on the concert, but he was adamant; the band's management was strict in granting access.

Now I was unsure how to fulfill my promise to my friends waiting outside the press gate. This situation now called for Plan B, but unfortunately, I had not developed one. The arena was on lockdown, and our forlorn group joined all the other hopefuls to walk the arena's perimeter.

Approximately fifty feet from the press gate, one of the doors magically opened in front of me. We dashed into the arena, and the fire door automatically closed behind us. Before we ventured along a hallway, I surveyed the area, and there was the press entrance security guard who winked. I acknowledged him with a broad smile; his timing was superb.

Around a corner, we were confronted by an unprepared security guard focused on the main entrance. Aghast and befuddled to encounter nine gate-crashers, we barreled past him in different directions to locate a place to watch the show. We climbed our own stairway to our heaven, elated to be a part of this historical event. The next day, the Washington Post accurately described the concert as "vintage Led Zeppelin". Whenever I hear *Stairway to Heaven*, it's a flashback to a phenomenal night. Unlike us, the lady in the song had to buy her way in!

Today, my friends regale our exploits, a few venues I barely recall, with amazement and laughter. Dozens of friends and I gained free entry to concerts, each one with a different tactic, and the methods employed were fond memories alongside the music.

The culmination of the 1960s music scene ended with the most historical music event in the world: Woodstock. There are thousands of stories focused on this unforgettable event and the music, so I will simply share my personal experience and perspective.

The Woodstock Music and Art Fair, informally known as the Woodstock Festival or simply Woodstock, occurred August 15th-17th, 1969 on Max Yasgur's dairy farm in the Catskill Mountains northwest of New York City. The festival was extended to Monday, August 18th after attracting an audience of over 400,000 young people and music lovers to the

600-acre dairy farm near the hamlet of White Lake in the town of Bethel in Sullivan County.

Thirty-two acts performed outdoors, and the event is widely regarded as a pivotal moment in popular music history. *Rolling Stone* listed it as one of the "50 Moments That Changed the History of Rock and Roll." The event was immortalized in the Academy Award-winning 1970 documentary movie *Woodstock*, and Joni Mitchell's song of the same name was a major hit for Crosby, Stills, Nash, and Young and for Matthews Southern Comfort. In 2017, the festival site was listed in the National Register of Historic Places.

The festival was constantly advertised on the radio as the premier event of the year. My two friends, Tulip and Michelle, suggested the three of us hitchhike to Woodstock. I happily agreed and appreciated hitchhiking with two attractive girls. I predicted a ride within a brief period, but I was wrong. Dozens of cars and trucks drove by, and an hour later I dejectedly sat on the side of the road on top of Tulip's makeup case, a mere three miles from home.

Eventually, two girls in a 1963 Rambler American convertible drove in our direction. I immediately deduced they were Woodstock bound and leapt into the air, feverishly waving my arms over my head. In doing so, I tripped over Tulip's case and fell on my butt. As I regained my footing, my face matching the color of my hair, the car waited, and the driver and passenger giggled uncontrollably. It was a small price to pay.

The two girls, Julie and Susie, were indeed going to Woodstock, traveling from Crofton, the neighboring town to Bowie. The five of us fit comfortably in their car, and as we headed north, we were full of anticipation and contagious enthusiasm. We sensed others were on the same pilgrimage as they left their jobs and homes to travel for hundreds of miles to participate in this once in a lifetime festival.

The conversation became lighthearted as we smoked hash. In our giddiness, we traded stories, experiencing one of those amazing 'small world' moments as Susie recounted a story from two years ago. Prompted by a discussion of the relative merits—or not—of Bowie, she mentioned her mother's visit to a Bowie art gallery.

Susie's mother planned to purchase a painting she admired. Upon her return a few days later, the gallery owner said a young man bought the painting to her bitter disappointment. To Susie's disbelief, I described the painting her mother adored since I was the buyer. The painting, which is in my bedroom today, depicts a contented French hobo on a bench with his bottle of wine and a cigarette.

The munchies surfaced, and our next stop was to buy ice cream cones at the first Howard Johnson service center on the New Jersey Turnpike. We approached the stereotypical gum-chewing waitress, her hair held in place in a bun with a well-chewed pencil, as she manned the cash register. As the girls dove into their ice cream cones, I offered to pay, when the waitress noticed my pained look.

"You going to Woodstock?" she asked and as we nodded, she added, "Well, you have a great time, and there is no charge for the ice cream."

We thanked her and merrily went on our way. This was our first hint of a monumental event unfolding prior to our arrival at the festival. The second occurred at a gas station close to the site.

There were dozens of empty soda boxes and cartons, stacked haphazardly along the wall, and this was another indication we were near the epicenter of something mammoth and unparalleled. This was during the days of full-service gas stations, and the attendants ran back and forth fueling four vehicles at a time.

We waited ten minutes for our turn, and as our tank was filled, the ecstatic gas station owner said he was concerned with his dwindling supply of gasoline after hundreds of customers. He was delirious with the day's volume of business and cheerfully gave us five free sodas from his remaining rapidly dwindling stock. He revealed Bethel, NY was normally a sleepy small town, and he had his best day of business by a significant margin. Once more, we sensed this was truly an epic event.

We joined the procession of hippie festival-goers as cars moved slowly in heavy traffic. The endless parade of hippie attendees was greeted by dozens of cheering residents lining the side of the road, throwing homemade cookies and handmade beaded rings into cars.

The shopkeepers busily helped customers who propelled their businesses to record-breaking sales. The depleted inventory was evidenced by the empty boxes piled high in front of their stores. The massive hippie invasion of Bethel was more than double the invasion of Normandy in World War II. It was 'H(ippie)-Day' for the astounded residents.

Woodstock was originally designed as a profit-making venture and famously became a free concert after the event attracted a far greater number of people than the organizers prepared for. Tickets for the three-day event were advertised at $18 in advance and $24 at the gate (equivalent to $120 and $160 today) and approximately 186,000 tickets were sold in advance. The organizers expected 200,000 festival-goers to attend, and in the end, the actual number was greater than twice the estimate.

The original venue—in Wallkill, NY—became problematic after residents rejected the idea. The Wallkill Zoning Board of Appeals officially banned the concert because "the planned portable toilets did not adhere to town code." This weak excuse was ridiculed in press reports of the ban, which led to a publicity bonanza for the festival.

Ideas for other venues were pursued unsuccessfully, encountering legal and permit issues, until the promoters were introduced to dairy farmer Max Yasgur. His land formed a natural bowl sloping downward to the bottom of a hill with a pond and this offered a perfect setting for the stage and a natural amphitheater. The pond, not surprisingly, became a popular skinny-dipping destination.

The late change of the venue impeded the ability of festival organizers to adequately prepare fencing and ticket booths causing lost income. With dwindling funds, their other option involved allocating their remaining resources toward building the stage or risk a disappointed and disgruntled audience. As the hordes of spectators descended by the tens of thousands, the decision was made for them. The organizers were forced to suspend ticket sales. Half of the total attendees, myself included, simply walked in.

The organizers later avoided bankruptcy through their ownership of the film and recording rights, which certainly compensated their losses after the release of the hit documentary film the following year. With an estimated budget of $600,000, to date, the film has grossed around $50,000,000 in the U.S. alone.

Despite recently relocating their commune to Llano, New Mexico, the famed hippie group known as the Hog Farmers accepted the offer to become involved with Woodstock. They were recruited to build fire pits and trails on the festival grounds and to manage security. The group was called the 'Please Force', a reference to their non-intrusive tactics at keeping order, for which they were successful in their 'please' loving job.

It was 8:00 p.m., on Thursday, the night before the event, when we arrived at Woodstock. The atmosphere and sense of anticipation were akin to a childhood Christmas morning for the tens of thousands of eager people on the festival grounds. As I said goodbye to Julie and Susie, Tulip and Michelle also disappeared into the crowd.

The bowl-shaped area in front of the stage was empty for the moment as I strolled slowly down the hill, intent on staking my claim to an ideal viewing spot. Within ten minutes, a vigilant security guard politely said the area was off limits until morning. For the next few hours, I basked in the ever-growing celebration before the first note of music. The convergence of music-loving pilgrims created an atomic explosion of hippies onto the landscape. Around the peripheries of the site, where people camped temporarily, the atmosphere was electric as the throngs of hippies laughed, sang, and danced.

Eventually, rest was a wise option to prepare for the next few days. I slept in a secluded wooded area between the stage and the Hog Farm commune. I awoke to another sunny morning; it was time to re-stake my claim to a spot in front of the stage. I tied my bedroll, grabbed my backpack, and scampered along, full of high hopes of reclaiming a grassy patch to partake in the music and merriment.

As I zealously reached the clearing, I incredulously blinked my eyes in disbelief at the arena. In the few hours I slept, tens of thousands of people had descended on the area. The sea of humanity stretched from the stage in all directions. To enter the arena of revelers surrounding the stage was as impossible as putting a girdle on a hippopotamus. The festive spectators, blankets, sleeping bags, tents, and coolers covered every square inch of space. Crowds of people camped in every direction from the stage as far as the eye could see, ready to party for the next three days as the music played on.

My disappointment was short-lived as I plopped on the grass in the first available spot. With my arms wrapped around my legs, I digested the scene. My heightened admiration for the festival organizers coincided with the realization they created a city-sized festival with hundreds of thousands of music lovers.

A tap on the shoulder interrupted my ponderings. It was Mike, one of my friends from Bowie! "Hey man!" I said as I leapt to my feet. "I didn't know you were here!"

"Me neither," he replied.

"Well, my hair is bright this morning," I said, and he laughed.

"I did see that first," he admitted. "There's a few of us from Bowie at the Hog Farm. Let's go!"

The Bowie contingent was close to where the camper school buses were parked; they were called magic buses by the Hog Farmers. The site was idyllic; a grassy meadow surrounded by trees and fewer campers. The Bowie gang camped by the edge of the meadow, near the portable toilets, water fountains, and the Hog Farm free kitchen, from which the Hog Farmers distributed free food buffet-style.

For the time we were all there, we happily survived on a main entree of brown rice and cabbage, in addition to a few other natural foods and fresh vegetables. Long lines formed quickly for the delectable food, and the Hog Farmers' contribution to feeding the hungry was a lifesaver for many of us. The other option for provisions required a long walk to town, missing whoever might be on stage.

Throughout the festival, I alternated my time between the entertainment on the main stage and our 'mini-Bowie' at the Hog Farm campsite. A small free stage was erected close to where my friends and I gathered, and this was available for both amateur and main acts to perform.

Joan Baez, six months pregnant at the time, sang for an audience of three dozen, including myself. Between songs, she proudly discussed her husband David Harris, a journalist and author who was in prison for refusing to be inducted into the U.S. Army. It was a remarkable performance of song and conversation in an intimate setting. She recounted how anti-Vietnam War protesters pasted a 'Resist the Draft' bumper sticker on the police car during Harris's arrest.

Wavy Gravy, the entertainer, peace activist, and co-founder of the Hog Farm, performed on the same stage. With his battered hillbilly hat and toothless grin, his magic tricks wowed the children who camped nearby.

The never-ending crescendo of people flooded in by the thousands, anxiously searching for a campsite as the festival began. The congestion peaked on Friday, culminating in the worst gridlock. The arena was crammed as people danced effortlessly around each other to locate a spot somewhere here or there.

American ingenuity was at work as primitive forms of communication were instituted. Signs on bulletin boards and notes on trees were effective means to reconnect lost friends and family. Before long, the sunny day changed to periods of rain and thunder, continuing off and on for the remainder of the festival, yet the inclement weather did not affect the mood of celebration and solidarity.

The Bowie group expanded to ten at our Hog Farm location, as friends explored the neighborhood and reconnected one by one. New friendships were formed with our camping neighbors. By Saturday night, our campsite boasted nearly one hundred chilled and wet folks. As more people gathered, crazy 'backflip' Kurt was hellbent on hosting the weekend's largest bonfire, and he ran back and forth into the forest to collect firewood to build his legacy. He had a grand time and became Lord of the Fire for the evening. Judging from the festive atmosphere all night around the continually roaring bonfire, he had achieved his McLuhanesque fifteen minutes of fame.

One night on the free stage, short speeches and announcements were heard on the open platform. During one of these, someone referred to 'motherf*****s' and a spectator rebutted him by saying folks had no right to call anyone such names. Then another spectator shouted, "My father was a motherf*****," eliciting cheers from the crowd.

We slept outside in the open meadow, exposed to the incessant rain, but the night still offered a few hours of rest despite the mud, cold, and water streaming under and by my bedroll. As bizarre as this may sound, the music and high spirits were unwavering. These 'downside' factors all became positive elements to the Woodstock equation, exemplified by Groovy Way. This was the trail through the woods from the Hog Farm to the stage, a quarter mile path decorated with brightly colored Christmas lights.

The daily routine of camp life was established. The frequent thunderstorms provided a shower for everyone. The lines for the portable toilets were short and quick. Important news was announced between performances on the main stage and information filtered by word of mouth. The tragic news was a young man died while he slept under a tractor. The farmer, unable to see the camper, tragically drove over him with his tractor. It was a heartbreaking accident and warnings were issued to be aware of unforeseen dangers like tractors. We sympathized with both parties.

It was close to impossible for everyone to concurrently hear the music from the main stage. The constant ebb and flow of fans along the outside perimeter allowed a brief opportunity to view their favorite bands. Crowd control was virtually self-managed, and we were left to our own devices. The only task of the Hog Farm security force was to help lost children.

My favorite bedroll was swallowed by the mud on the second day, forever lost. I was not the solo victim. Thousands of blankets and sleeping bags became engulfed by the brown sludge, abandoned in the meadows and fields by the festival's end. A sleeping bag graveyard was born, which may be a fitting title for a Frank Zappa song.

Woodstock was the natural platform to scrub our souls from the traumatic events of the '60s. The country was fractured between the new and old guard, and Woodstock provided a safe harbor. The newfound hope of my generation to follow our dreams was evident, particularly by a guy named Steve who declared, "I am not leaving this place. I will live here for the rest of my life."

Woodstock was pivotal in diverse ways. Lifelong friendships and relationships were formed. Others developed inner strength to survive the rain, mud, lack of food, and limited facilities. The venue helped create a foundation of unparalleled resilience and enthusiasm for many souls. Music, nature, and thousands of people converged on the same track of life for a brief time. In our innocence, Woodstock provided the answers to our questions at the time. This fresh spirit of discovery ignited the light bulb moment for many: "So this is what life is all about."

It was a miracle this event happened at all, and the feeling of dreams coming true permeated the festival. The elation for everyone, which manifested itself in an army of smiling, laughing, clapping, and dancing hippies was not dampened by the weather, nor could it be attributed to drugs. A music festival of this magnitude was unprecedented, and the magical aura was infectious. 'Cosmic' and 'far out' aptly described the overall Woodstock experience.

The countless humans who descended en masse were enveloped in a mystical realm. The spirit of the festival on Max Yasgur's farm created a new foundation for making a difference in the world. Opportunity was everywhere, and the bands and performers were one part of an exceptional formula in the chain of events unfolding during those three 'event-full' days.

The inconsequential coincidences were forever life-changing. The building blocks of a life plan formed in my mind and prospered. It is difficult to define for everyone individually when this light bulb moment occurred but, in some way, the switch was turned on. We left the Woodstock Music Festival as new and improved versions of ourselves.

The fans funnel out during the Monday morning rush hour. The music was scheduled to finish in the early hours of the morning, but the last note was played at 11:10 a.m. I choose to linger to avoid the mass exodus.

Similar to Steve, my procrastination prolongs my departure from this magical place. Rather than joining the bedraggled crowds filing out, I head in the opposite direction from the Hog Farm towards the main music stage. The incredible joy I had upon my arrival remains intact.

The meadows and fields are slowly reborn to their natural state. The excitement is slipping away as workers collect trash, blankets, sleeping bags, and debris. Nothing will erase the memories buried deep in the soil of the farm, beneath the meadows that were transformed for a few days into what will become one of the most iconic events in history.

The smell of fresh coffee is in the air as the caffeine races through my veins. The same is happening to everyone else. As if poured into coffee cups to bring sustenance, the rain and mud are the launch pads for an enhanced outlook. We taste the perfect espresso with the sweetest crema and aroma—it is called life without boundaries, a delightful elixir transforming us in ways no one could ever anticipate.

I am fortunate to be one of the remaining spectators. The arena is empty except for a few hundred people who watch and listen to Jimi Hendrix perform his signature rendition of the Star-Spangled Banner. Procrastination makes a nation, and in this case, leads to witnessing an unprecedented performance without crowds. Let the sunshine in!

TRACK NINE

CANNED HEAT: GOING UP THE COUNTRY

Afterwards, despite being buoyed by Woodstock, my past still haunted me. My albatrosses are high anxiety flashbacks. At the onset of each episode, the initial step was to identify the emotion, "Was this from my past or present?" Often, it was reminiscent of drowning in an ocean of doubt.

My panic attacks are unpredictable, and each one is unique in intensity and duration. The best description is extreme pain in my stomach and back, combined with a colossal fear of immediate death at the hands of faceless goblins. I honed my coping skills by directing the added adrenaline to accomplish more in a single day.

This was a helpful tactic to alleviate the disruption of these wild, overwhelming emotions until they subsided. I managed to attain a sense of normalcy within a few hours although sometimes, poor decisions were made based on misinformation from my emotional roller-coaster. Wave after wave of fear with each attack was followed by the hammer of anxiety.

The pressure related to high anxiety generally leads a frightened individual to withdraw to 'safe zones', usually at home. I avoided this since my constant urge to travel outweighed the fear of more attacks, and my friends provided helpful suggestions.

One night, the anxiety increased to overwhelming proportions at a party. My friend Wayne handed me an anti-depressant pill and provided no other details. In my desperation to relieve the nightmare, I swallowed one and then thirty minutes later, another. Pow! The full force of the hammer crashed down, and I lost consciousness.

In today's world, my friends may have suspected an overdose, but instead I was carried to Sammy's car. It was the following afternoon before I opened my eyes and found my head on a pretty girl's lap, amazed my limp body wasn't dropped or injured as it was maneuvered into the car. When I questioned where the hell we were going, the answer was New York City for the weekend. This was their naïve expectation of my ability to sleep it off. I did, but I guess I was lucky.

> *It is raining, and the wind is blowing outside the car window. It is perfect weather to fly in an airplane. My mantra is any day or time is an opportunity to travel. My friends now call me Ron Vacation. I am the one who travels and spreads the news about new places and ideas. I regale them with tales of having fun on the road, but not this day, as I wonder how close I was to death.*

> *"Good morning to you, Father Time. Is it my time to shine?"*

> *"Look far and wide, and what do you see, young man?" replies Father Time.*

> *"The future!" I answer.*

> *"You are smart. I have witnessed all of eternity. Be thankful for all of life's suffering and catastrophes. This is something integral to your survival in the world," says Father Time.*

"How can this be? Suffering and catastrophes are painful. Your formula is flawed, you wait and see!" I say defiantly. "Look at you, look at me. I walk the walk and talk the talk."

"Do you see the joy in having your pants on fire? The urgency increases with the pain. It is the best motivator," advises Father Time.

"I want to see all that was and will be," I reply.

"Open the door, and you will see the future. Close the door, and all you will see is the past. You shall choose the future; that is my answer," are his final words.

A lapse in judgment loses sight of all that awaits. This lesson occurred after a casual remark to my friend Fred. One morning in September '69, I spoke with Fred as I exited the bank in Bowie with five hundred dollars in cash. This was withdrawn to retain a lawyer for my arrest for possession of marijuana.

This incident began when a few friends and I were in a car one night, and my friend Buddy was the driver. In his pocket was a small plastic sandwich bag containing three or four grams of marijuana. In the event we were stopped by the police—a common occurrence when long hair was in view—the plan was to throw the plastic bag out the window.

We were close to our destination when Buddy noticed a police car with flashing lights in his rear-view mirror. In a panic, he handed the bag to me which I threw out the window. We breathed a collective sigh of relief, as Buddy coasted to the side of the road without a care in the world. The first bombshell was when none other than my nemesis Officer H. sauntered to our car. The second whammy was when he arrested us for possession of marijuana.

Gravity was reversed by a fickle wind of fate as the plastic baggie gracefully flew through the air before landing squarely on Officer

H.'s windshield. As he read us our rights, he struggled to contain his amusement with this chain of events. At the police station, the comical aspect of what transpired was evident in his ever-present beaming grin as he happily typed his report. We failed to see the humor in the matter until the case was dismissed in court.

Our hysterical caper occurred four months after Timothy Leary's case was heard for the same offense, but his transgression reached the Supreme Court. He was detained by customs officers in Laredo, Texas as he drove from Mexico. Five ounces of marijuana were found in his car, and he was arrested for illegal possession under the Marijuana Tax Act of 1937. It was a routine arrest, and an opportunity for Leary, who welcomed a national drug debate.

After several appeals, when *Leary v. the United States* was heard, Americans were forced—for the first time—to reckon with the prejudices and assumptions behind drug legislation. Leary's victory set little legal precedent, the only factor being the way in which he won—with the logic absent from the process of writing the law. Leary argued the Marijuana Tax Act violated the Fifth Amendment since it forced him to self-incriminate when he admitted to possession of drugs.

It was a minor victory for the Bill of Rights, but by 1970, the law was replaced by the Comprehensive Drug Abuse Prevention and Control Act. Today, we are working under the same framework, specifically the portion now known as the Controlled Substances Act. This Act lists marijuana as a Schedule One substance, meaning Congress believes it has "no currently accepted medical use" and a high potential for addiction and abuse.

The consensus is this stance is misguided, refuted by dozens of scientific studies which prove the medical benefits of marijuana. The legislators of twenty-three states also legalized it for varying degrees of medicinal and recreational use.

During our initial conversation, my attorney was confident of a not guilty verdict. I expected the whole ordeal to conclude in a couple of weeks, and all in all, the day I had my appointment with the attorney was a pleasant day.

With spare time before my appointment, I ambled to the Freestate Mall—not the one I was banned from—and crossed paths with two acquaintances named Wally and Sherman. The mall was quiet, and we anticipated more friends arriving shortly. In the interim, Wally suggested smoking pot, and we headed into the woods behind the mall parking lot.

At our hidden location in the trees behind a fence, we sat down to smoke. Well, this was my understanding. Wally removed his hand from his pocket, and instead of firing up a joint, he was ready to fire at me with his handgun. I was bewildered by this unexpected sequence of events. This was a valuable lesson to just say no to drugs.

"Give me the money, Ron," Wally said quite casually as if asking for a match.

"What money?" I asked, attempting to sound casual too.

"You took 500 bucks out of the bank this morning."

"How did ..."

"Fred told me."

I reclined on my elbows and replied, "Wally, you're too late. I don't have the money. Your timing stinks. Let's smoke and forget about it."

"I don't have any pot. I just want your money," Wally retorted, and I rose to my feet.

"Well, see you later," I said and walked off.

Their only motive was to commit robbery, and I presumed since we met by accident, my involvement was unintended. In the future, I'll know it's a gun in his pocket and he's not happy to see me. Wally was unaware the money remained in my pocket. My attorney was paid, and another crisis was averted.

There is a short learning curve in understanding the character of casual friends. The betrayal when money is involved is swift, and it was unnecessary to arrest someone for stupidity. I was confident the authorities would handle this in the future. While Bowie was not quite Dodge City, I felt the desire to leave town for a while to meet four friends—honest and reliable ones—Richie, Rick, Perry, and Stan in pre-Disney World Orlando.

In 1969, the Orlando airport was small and provincial in contrast to its rank today as the thirteenth busiest airport in the U.S. Its initial nickname 'The City Beautiful' was exemplified by its well-manicured streets and parks. The sleepy days of Orlando ended with the opening of Walt Disney World in October 1971, ushering in rapid growth in population and economy. Its second nickname 'Theme Park Capital of the World' aptly describes the city now, one of the most popular tourist destinations in the world.

This was my first visit to the city, where my four friends and I were popular with plenty of girls. We became celebrities, yet unaware of our 'rock star' status. I later determined the reason was attributed to our hippie appearance. While the first generation of counterculture pioneers was hated by many, it was only a few months after Woodstock, and we were admired by others, a category which included many teenage girls.

As Richie and I explored to find something new, it was the reverse, and we were discovered. Wherever we went, attractive girls clamored to our side, and the rest was left to nature; we did what came naturally. Richie and I also spent time in our apartment with new friends and neighbors, discussing life and how we saw the future unfolding. We did not want to follow the conventional lifestyle of our parents and grandparents. Our common goal was to live our youth in our own way, immune to the expectations of our elders and society at large.

Between the five of us and a continuing stream of guests, our apartment was as full as our pantry was usually bare. Our other three roommates lived modestly while Richie and I worked odd jobs during the day. We pooled our earnings, and after a particularly prosperous week, had nearly one hundred dollars, equivalent to six hundred dollars today. Richie and I rushed to the Winn-Dixie supermarket to buy food for everyone in the apartment.

I was ecstatic and drooling in the store aisles, my taste buds alive with anticipation as we filled the shopping cart. One by one, beaming brighter than a pair of lighthouse beacons, we placed our favorite items into the cart—steak, ground beef, chicken, bread, and pretzels. We were truly kids in a candy store, running wild to feed ourselves and our friends. As we grabbed food from the shelves aisle by aisle, we attracted the attention of other grocery shoppers to the point where a few started following us.

We guessed a full shopping cart amounted to one hundred dollars, which could easily feed several families for a week. As the cashier totaled our groceries, another couple watched as our items moved along the conveyor and they complimented us on our shopping expertise. By the time our bounty was bagged, we had $14.00 remaining.

With change in hand and a stack of Green Stamps, the middle-aged couple behind us requested our Green Stamps and we obliged. Supermarkets during that period offered these stamps as a bonus, one of the first retail loyalty programs, enticing customers to become frequent shoppers. Customers collected the stamps in paper booklets, which were redeemed for various merchandise once the booklets were full.

As we exited, Richie gave me a sly look as he suggested we take the shopping cart to avoid carrying the groceries. "Go ahead. I'll pass,"

I said. He laughed, and while it was a struggle to juggle the bags, we gleefully brought our groceries home. A week or two worth of food filled our bare pantry and refrigerator.

Heroes to our roommates and new friends, it was a veritable food orgy for a mere two days before the pantry and refrigerator were empty. It was a fun food-filled time, and Richie and I laughed at our gastronomic marathon, surrounded by bulging bellies.

Several weeks later, a photographer from the *Orlando Sentinel* was searching for a hippie for the front page of their Sunday Parade magazine. I was referred by a friend at the newspaper and was chosen for the photo shoot. The published photo two weeks later cemented my rock star status among the girls in the neighborhood and the parties, music concerts, and festivals multiplied. It was the wildest time of my life until the strangest of circumstances drastically changed my perspective.

The national initiative, supported by every U.S. police department, to eradicate hippies from the landscape was now in full force.

In the car belonging to our friend John, we waited while he, being twenty-two, purchased a thirty-two-ounce bottle of beer for himself at a convenience store. The moment he returned to his vehicle, a policeman leaped from his patrol car parked near us and immediately demanded the contents of John's bag.

The policeman radioed a fellow officer for backup, and within five minutes, the second officer was on the scene to view the prize catch of the day ... me. The lone hippie in the car, at age twenty, I was a year away from drinking legally.

The two officers chuckled for a few minutes before I was placed under arrest for possession of alcohol due to the lone, unopened bottle of beer. My three other underage friends with shorter hair were ignored. An unpleasant night in jail coupled with the fifty-dollar bond payment in the morning led me to conclude it was time to leave Orlando.

The absurdity of my arrest was beyond the sphere of comprehension. Is it possible this police department had a contest for hippie arrests? Yes, this week only, the winner will receive two round-trip plane tickets to the Bahamas. The funny grand prizes the two policemen deserved to win for their capture of this fine hippie specimen swirled in my mind. Two months earlier, my four roommates were arrested for disturbing the peace; their radio was too loud. Which one of our arrests was the most ridiculous? It was a close contest.

Shortly before I left, another fond memory during my time in Orlando was added with a noteworthy story concerning our friend Vince from Paterson, NJ. At 5'7" and 145 pounds, Vince was stocky, yet unassuming and his personality was cordial and friendly. After exchanging a few pleasantries when we met on the street, with a modest smile, he said, "I had an unusual time in a bar last night."

"What happened?" I asked.

Vince described being in a bar in Kissimmee, sipping his beer and munching on peanuts when an aggressive tap on his shoulder disturbed his peace and quiet. A large redneck angrily stated, "I know you're a queer."

"Yes, you're right. I am a homosexual," Vince responded cheerfully. "Let's go to the parking lot, and I'll blow you and your two friends. Go first, and I'll follow you."

The three rednecks gaily strutted out the back door. As Vince followed, he grabbed a full pot of coffee from the warmer close to the exit. He flew out the back door and flung hot coffee on the first redneck, smashed the coffee pot over the second one's head, and kicked the third firmly between his legs. Vince proceeded to wallop the three bewildered guys until they were no longer a threat.

"That was my night out," Vince concluded as if nothing much happened. "What's new with you?"

Later in life, I mused whether Lee Child spoke with Vince concerning his ideas for the scenes where ex-MP Jack Reacher is similarly outnumbered. Vince's story also illustrates why diminutive Tom Cruise was an appropriate choice to play the hero in the movies.

Upon returning to Bowie, the latest development on how to avoid the U.S. military unfolded thanks to my mother. The aftermath of the Baltimore Four court case resulted in a bureaucratic backlog of epic proportions, while the Vietnam War escalated with no end in sight. My brilliant mother concluded the U.S. Army did not deserve her son when she persuaded the psychiatrist my serving in the U.S. Army was detrimental to her mental health.

I optimistically contacted the draft board to relay her psychiatrist's recommendation. The clerk's instructions were to send the psychiatrist's letter to her office and a deferment would be granted. As I slowly placed the handset on its cradle, the years of concern regarding combat in Vietnam for a lost cause ended. I sat in silence for a few minutes and smiled. One brief phone call, and I avoided Vietnam.

TRACK TEN

CREEDENCE CLEARWATER REVIVAL: HAVE YOU EVER SEEN THE RAIN

In the first days of January 1970, my New Year's resolution was to have a breakthrough year. This period was relatively calm for me in Orlando as I formulated the idea of a world tour. I intended to travel the traditional route through Europe and on to Asia, and I spent time planning a route and studying the countries on my wish list. I returned to Bowie in mid to late February, hopefully a brief stop before Europe.

At the time, the political acrimony and social disharmony in the U.S. was a further impetus to travel abroad.

For instance, in February 1970, Jeffrey R. MacDonald murdered his wife and children at Fort Bragg, North Carolina, and claimed drugged-out hippies committed the crime. This fueled the establishment's propaganda machine to spew additional venom towards the counterculture.

In the same month, a jury found the defendants known as the Chicago Seven not guilty of conspiring to incite a riot; their charges stemmed from the violence in 1968 at the Democratic National Convention. Five of the defendants were found guilty on the lesser charge of crossing state lines to incite a riot.

In March, a bomb constructed by members of the Weathermen and meant to be planted at a military dance in New Jersey exploded prematurely, killing three members of the organization. Also, in March, the U.S. Army charged fourteen officers with suppressing information related to the dreadful My Lai massacre in Vietnam two years before when hundreds of unarmed civilians and children were killed.

Life in the U.S. was further fractured with two major political wings of the left and the right being poles apart for their own benefit, and not for their electorates. Meanwhile, the campaign to pressure baby boomers to conform to the status quo prevailed. The anti-war protesters and pro women's liberation, free choice, birth control, and abortions were subjected to the snapping whips of the lion tamers.

On April 10th, I was disappointed to read in the morning newspaper Paul McCartney's announcement of The Beatles disbanding. My disheartened mood was lifted on the next page by an airline advertisement—an Icelandic Airlines flight from New York City to Luxembourg for $178 one way. My dream of circling the world was reignited.

It was a dismal, rainy morning as I visualized baguettes, croissants, and smiling mademoiselles in France, a short hitchhike from Luxembourg. I boarded a bus from Baltimore to New York City and on to JFK airport. My thoughts were to roam Europe beginning with Paris as the first stop.

I checked in with high hopes and without a plane ticket. Icelandic Airlines was known for the lowest airfares, yet it was possible an enticing airfare might arise from another airline. A cheaper airfare was elusive, and the Icelandic Airlines ticket counter was busier than Walmart on Black Friday.

In line for a ticket to Luxembourg, another traveler on his way from the ticket counter remarked, "I'm #17 for standby." Desperate to flee, eventually I became standby passenger #35. This entailed 35 passengers canceling their reservation before my opportunity to board the plane. It was foolish on my part to believe there was a cheaper deal. The odds were not in my favor since the average number of cancellations is only eight to ten per flight.

The weather that day was dreary. The rain progressed into an ongoing thunderstorm, and this was our distraction as ticketed passengers were called for boarding. The first ten standby numbers were announced for seat assignments, and I resigned myself to sleeping in the airport. The two dozen or so hardy standby passengers ahead of me in the queue prayed for their number to be called. The procedure of calling five standbys in sequence became nerve-wracking.

The departure lounge was eerily quiet in between claps of thunder as other prospective passengers and I shared "so what number are you?" in a game of standby bingo. The weather impacted the number of no-shows. The bingo standby numbers bounced in uncertainty for me and the last four in the departure lounge. BINGO! Despite a plethora of no-show passengers, the flight was sold out, and we, the final five, were called to board. Bingo became **B**oarding **I**s **N**ow **G**et **O**n.

The turboprop plane was a four-engine Vickers Viscount, and my seat assignment was adjacent to the two props on the port side. Introduced in 1948, this aircraft was well-received by the flying public since its cabin conditions provided reductions in vibration and noise. Regardless, the 'symphony' of the four propellers for the next fifteen hours was a character-building experience for myself and my seatmates. Although the noise and vibrations were nuisances, the price was right. Note to my future self: Jets will be preferred over turboprops for all travel. Whatever the downside, I was en route to Luxembourg, a short distance from Paris, and my Eiffel Tower state of mind was closer.

There was a brief stop in Reykjavik to refuel. As I meandered on the tarmac in my discombobulated state, I listened intently for the quiet sounds of glaciers in the distance, enjoying a brief respite before the last leg of the flight. Upon landing in Luxembourg, an extra dose of jet lag was countered by my adrenaline rush of being in Europe to hitchhike a mere four hours to Paris-dise, a fitting conclusion to my twenty-four-hour marathon.

Outside Luxembourg airport, I hitchhiked with my forefinger extended instead of my thumb as this was the accepted manner to hitchhike. In some European countries, an extended thumb is perceived as an obscene gesture. Shortly, a Citroen pulled alongside containing three other Americans, Sam, Joan, and Charlie who had been on the same flight from NYC. They had met at the baggage carousel while picking up their luggage and Sam invited Joan and Charlie for company in his rental car. I missed the early opportunity for a ride because of my carry-on luggage. Nevertheless, they stopped for me, and I occupied the fourth seat in this comfortable sedan.

Our reasons for being there differed, and Joan's was the most compelling. Her wedding day was two days ago in Illinois. At the church, Joan, her family, and friends gathered for the celebration and her emotional mother considered baby names for her future grandchildren. Her teary-eyed father prepared to escort Joan down the aisle. The missing link was her tardy fiancé. His last-minute phone call was earth shattering. He would not be attending the wedding. This cataclysmic news obliterated her future plans, and the next day, Joan abandoned her life in Illinois and embarked on a solo honeymoon.

It was hard to fathom Joan's nightmare. A well-educated, attractive woman left at the altar. She chose to travel to cleanse her soul rather than cry in her bedroom for the next five or ten years. With a one-way ticket, Joan laid the first bricks for rebuilding her life by touring the marvels of Europe. Sam and Charlie had more 'concrete' reasons for visiting Paris, but Joan and I were two wandering souls, potentially lost among the masses. We were examples of the old cliché of people seeking to find themselves, and our commonalities were a natural attraction.

It was comical to watch Sam direct his best romantic efforts toward Joan who was unimpressed by his amorous advances. Nevertheless, before we said our goodbyes at the Champs-Elysees, Sam's generous nature led to an evening tour of the illuminated streets and monuments of downtown Paris and the Eiffel Tower.

The May '68 student uprising and general strike which briefly paralyzed the city of Paris had a profound impact on French society. The five faculties of the University of Paris, founded in the 12th century, were broken up into thirteen independent campuses, and the streets around the university were no longer paved with cobblestones. These had been used extensively in the building of barricades.

Furthermore, President de Gaulle proposed a major restructuring of the French regions, and a reduction of power of the French Senate, and put his plan to vote in a national referendum, promising to resign if it did not pass. All the opposition parties, and many within de Gaulle's own party, opposed the change, and this was his downfall. This was Paris under President Georges Pompidou, previously de Gaulle's Prime Minister.

"Paris must adapt to the automobile," President Pompidou declared, and the French capital I witnessed was the burgeoning one of today. Owning an automobile became a status symbol celebrated in the French cinema, and they became ubiquitous to the point of parking cars on sidewalks. However, the French state built only 29 kilometers of highways, and none of the new roads entered the center of the city.

Charlie and Sam disappeared, while Joan and I, new kindred spirits, smiled at each other. In the heat of the moment, our passions propelled us to a quaint old Parisian hotel with a bathtub the size of the Citroen. This was our home for the next few days. Joan and I entertained each other as we sipped espresso into the night, visited the Eiffel Tower, and admired the Mona Lisa.

I am you, and you are me. This cannot be. I agree between you and me, there are similarities. Believe me, to be here today is truly unique. I look into your eyes. Baby, I love your eyes. You are me, and I am you. Some say it is Utopia.

Let's tiptoe among the dandelions and be fancy free as one intertwined organism embracing the tree of life. Let's hold hands as we cross the bridge over the cold brook. You and me is all that we'll be until we see the other side of life. Is this the best day ever? I am you, and you are me. Two carefree souls in the meadow.

Let's go to our little private espresso bar. I will prepare the beans for the coffee, my favorite elixir that imitates life. You will sit expectantly, imagining the aromas, taste and style captured within your cappuccino while I extract the goodness from the delectable coffee beans. The milk will soon be frothy, cascading on to the coffee goodness. Take a sip between you and me.

The love you feel will soon flow, building with intensity after each sip. First numbness, followed by euphoria, you proclaim "This is Utopia in a cup!" You and me, side by side, sipping the day away.

It was a glorious start for us, and we mutually attempted to heal our souls. Joan's emotions were frozen from the canceled wedding, but life is all about timing, and our meeting was opportune. It was a brief affair, and I was certain Joan's strength would prevail over her tragedy. Unfortunately for us, the effects of the anxiety pulverizing me had the upper hand.

My past lurked closer than a creature in a horror movie creeping around the corner preparing to pounce. I heard goblins knocking at the door, and the dizzying effect of the trauma, unbeknownst to me, ruled my decisions. The gong in my head sounded, and I said goodbye to Joan when uncontrollable emotions caused my departure to Israel. With my last $75 dollars, I boarded a flight to Tel Aviv and intended, once again, to work on a kibbutz. I was accepted on Sha'ar HaAmakim near Haifa.

Slightly under sixty miles north along the coast from Tel Aviv, the port city of Haifa is the third largest in Israel. Built in tiers extending from the Mediterranean to the north slope of Mount Carmel, the city's most iconic sites are the immaculately landscaped terraces of the Bahá'í Gardens and, at their heart, the gold-domed Shrine of the Báb. This location has a history spanning more than 3,000 years, with a small port city established in the late Bronze Age.

I was among other backpackers contemplating future fun as we worked in the orchards, chicken houses, cotton fields, and kitchen. The schedule of work in the morning and free time in the afternoon was a prescription for a carefree life. Room and board were provided for the thirty or so volunteers living there, and the work was hard, but rewarding.

It was entertaining to listen to several American volunteers pining for Coca-Cola. Their withdrawal from sugar and caffeine seemed to encompass their thoughts as fast foods were missed. However, new friends from around the world each added a new dimension.

I strived to absorb all the diverse cultural nuances in languages, expressions, behaviors, and customs, fascinated by the subtle variations from country to country. For example, in the United Kingdom, a car trunk is called a boot, a hood is a bonnet, and a fender is a bumper; the list goes on. The conversations and parties were nonstop, and we were all in the prime of our lives. Romance was short, educational, and limited only by our imagination.

In July, I heard the heartbreaking news of the shooting at Kent State University in May during a mass anti-Vietnam War protest. Twenty-nine guardsmen fired approximately sixty-seven rounds in thirteen seconds, killing four students and wounding nine others, one of whom suffered permanent paralysis.

One witness was Chrissie Hynde, the future lead singer of The Pretenders and a student at Kent State University at the time. I read her autobiography *Reckless: My Life as a Pretender* in 2015 where she described, with tremendous poignancy, what she saw:

> Then I heard the tatatatatatatatatat sound. I thought it was fireworks. An eerie sound fell over the common. The quiet felt like gravity pulling us to the ground. Then a young man's voice: "They f***ing killed somebody!" Everything slowed down, and the silence got heavier.
>
> The ROTC building, now nothing more than a few inches of charcoal, was surrounded by National Guardsmen. They were all on one knee and pointing their rifles at...us! Then they fired.
>
> By the time I made my way to where I could see them it was still unclear what was going on. The guardsmen themselves looked stunned. We looked at them and they looked at us. They were just kids, 19 years old, like us. But in uniform. Like our boys in Vietnam.

At the end of July, my world closer to home was jolted once more when I received two letters from the U.S. In the first, I read of two devastating tragedies involving close friends from Bowie. Craig died in an accident on his way to work when another vehicle rammed into the side of his car at a stop sign. Then, while in the Dominican Republic, Joe and his wife Kelly were murdered as their house burned. The newspaper reports speculated the cause was a sour business deal, but whatever the circumstances, all three were only in their twenties when their lives abruptly ended.

The second letter contained disturbing news concerning my friends Jim and Sherry. They were murdered on the porch of their newly purchased farm in Georgia. I met this lovely couple while I was living in Orlando. After Sherry inherited close to a million dollars, they chose to retire to

Athens, GA. Jim's hippie looks may have precipitated his death. Jim and Sherry were also in their early twenties when their lives were ended by a shotgun wielded by an unknown assailant. My hope, with this mention of their deaths five decades later, is their memories will somehow live on.

This horrendous news only reinforced my conviction of it being wiser to be a moving target, and travel was the answer. The camaraderie on the kibbutz was ideal, although as the world spun, so did I. Deeply saddened by the disturbing news, I landed on high anxiety. It was time for musical chairs. Once more, I needed to mosey, my wanderlust unmistakably insatiable.

I spoke with Sheila from Liverpool—it was she who explained the vagaries of car parts—as we ate dinner. She mentioned the imminent Isle of Wight pop festival in England at the end of August. It was an appealing suggestion to consider and all it amounted to was hitchhiking across Europe. The cheapest one-way ticket was $35 for a flight to Athens from Tel Aviv. After the cost of the plane ticket, I landed in Athens with ten dollars in my pocket.

My final destination was the Isle of Wight in England to attend the music festival at the end of August. I hoped to earn money working in Rotterdam to further my travels. The scuttlebutt among the kibbutz volunteers was that jobs were available on the docks in Rotterdam.

TRACK ELEVEN

MUDDY WATERS:
WALKING THROUGH THE PARK

O ften, hitchhiking involves sleeping outdoors, and the art of camping without a tent entails creative methods for a good night's sleep. The preferred lodging for backpackers was youth hostels at two dollars per night, but this was a luxury beyond my budget. Thus, I traveled with a bedroll or sleeping bag and the addition of a ground sheet is an effective barrier from Mother Earth.

The consequence for a night without a ground sheet is a cold night's sleep, regularly interrupted by trembles and shivers. Woodstock was my apprenticeship for sleeping in lousy weather. The cold, wet rain and mud there were my basic training for later travels. It provided a baseline with which to judge comfort and misery.

The places where I chose to rest were varied, ranging from the side of the road, under the bridges of interstate highways, on the roofs of buildings, in cemeteries, under trees, on beaches, in cars, sidewalks, and lounge chairs. All provided a place for a weary hippie to lay his head.

For instance, it was straightforward to traipse fifty feet from the road into a meadow in the Yugoslavian countryside and slumber for the evening. The difficulty increased within cities or near military bases, and Belgrade proved no exception. The welcome sign in front of one military base prominently warned: 'Take a photo and go to jail'.

My first introduction to a Communist country from within was vaguely familiar. Although governments are different, humans are humans, and citizens everywhere are similar. The typical local attire for men were light blue shirts and dark blue pants. Women wore simple dresses in like colors. The blank expressions on people's faces as they trudged to work during morning and evening rush hour were identical to the faces of residents in any other large city.

People curiously stared at the long-haired stranger in their midst. In some respect, behaviors are identical throughout the world. The workers with unfulfilled desires glared at me with a sense of envy. As a lone backpacker, I maneuvered past the drudgery of my fellow pedestrians. I was living the dream, albeit on a small budget. They had a place to sleep, food and family, but as a tourist, I was unchained. My adventurous way of life was apparent, and the monotony of a routine life was crystal clear.

It was now evening, and my objective was to locate a suitable place to sleep for the night. A quiet cemetery was my first choice. It is a peaceful place for a backpacker to rest—but proved elusive due to the congestion of buildings and people.

Lost and sleepy after wandering for hours in Belgrade, I saw treetops on the horizon bordering a large park. A similar place in Paris, close to the Eiffel Tower, was a convenient place to bed down for days without incident.

This park was a popular evening destination, and a quiet, serene haven within the otherwise bustling city. It was filled to capacity, as though all its citizens pounced at once to escape their gray, concrete socialist housing blocks, where the sidewalks were crammed in every direction.

The park was the place for everyone to be seen and to mingle with friends as little children ran with merriment in front of their parents, happy to be outside. Couples smiled at each other, grateful to have a moment together among the throngs of like-minded neighbors. I speculated few residents owned a television, and the park served as the evening entertainment venue.

Belgrade is delightful, especially its park, but it was sleep I craved. In the center of the park, every street lamp was at its brightest. It was nighttime, yet the lights shone brighter than the sun. In their midst, I was the sailor in the crow's nest peering across the sea for a safe harbor. And I found one!

My favorite is what I refer to as my five-star Belgrade bush. It was in the middle of Belgrade's central park, adjacent to a pedestrian sidewalk, where mothers pushed baby strollers, cyclists pedaled, and lovers walked hand in hand. They all promenaded past the five-star bush which had escaped the Michelin list.

She was a wonderful specimen of shrubbery, ten feet across, with thousands of interlocking leaves forming a perfect globe in the center of the park's gardens. This was a chance meeting, and my wish was answered. The lovely, all-natural, green tent was my refuge for the night. She was unnoticed by the promenading crowds as they walked and talked. She was ignored by all except me, and I was in love.

My next step was to find an entrance into the interior of the bush and become as invisible as my lovely shrubbery. Two sides of the bush abutted the sidewalks, and behind, she was protected by stout trees and three smaller neglected bushes. I rejected slow, meticulous actions and lunged into her with wanton abandonment.

Inside, she was akin to a green and brown igloo, with a well-developed interior free from obtrusive branches. There was a smooth king-sized dirt floor and a four-foot dome. My view from the bush was the endless march of shoes and more shoes, and as I fell asleep, it was as if she wrapped her arms around me.

The bush was my home for two nights, and the fond memories of this illustrious piece of shrubbery are part of the unexpected joys of a backpacker. The small and unexpected pleasures are hidden in plain sight, invisible to others.

As I trekked to Rotterdam, the ride from Belgrade was with two American college students, Alan and Ben, who were touring Europe. They occasionally bickered, and hitchhikers were buffers and distractions. The second passenger in the car was Moe, the Surgeon General of Tunisia. My burning question was his reason for hitchhiking, and Moe replied surgeon generals were poorly compensated in Tunisia.

As we left the city, in front of the same military base from a few days ago, Alan stopped for two hitchhikers from Australia. Rupert was an aboriginal, and Russell was a white Australian. Their ordeal to obtain a ride had so far lasted five days, but for Rupert, it did not end. Upon being informed there was room for only one additional passenger, Russell immediately jumped in and slammed the door, leaving Rupert behind. Russell introduced himself as a draft dodger traveling in Europe, adding a new dimension to the unusual cast of characters under one car roof.

The scenery, as we cruised through the Alps, was breathtaking, with impressive mountains soaring into the sky. Several times, Alan's vehicle had insufficient power to ascend the steepest segments of the Alps. Each time this occurred, Alan drove, and we followed on foot while the car slowly chugged up the mountain. The hills were alive with visions of the Von Trapp family singing and dancing as we walked. After passing the crest of each mountain peak, the four of us hopped into the car.

We parted in Salzburg. Our paths crossed in our travels, where fleeting moments were shared and, as with car companions, it is difficult to know what became of them. Perhaps Moe's salary increased, and Rupert was eventually rescued. We adventurers followed our different highways with high hopes. For myself, I was optimistic to be in Rotterdam soon.

It was not an easy journey through Germany. The old expression, "When times are tough, the tough get going," is steeped in truth. Hunger is a wonderful motivator for me when food and sustenance are absent. Creativity accelerates as the perfect counter-balance and, on many occasions, the universe and my stomach worked in tandem to resolve the most pressing dilemmas.

I was stranded on a highway outside of Frankfurt in a torrential downpour. I was ravenously hungry, not having eaten since breakfast, but it was also a cool night, and my priority was shelter before food. As the aroma of Frankfurter sausages wafted over the horizon, a truck park sign illuminated the darkness, providing sudden inspiration.

A parked truck with a canvas enclosure was an inviting sight, and I climbed aboard and soon fell asleep despite my bedraggled state. In the morning, I was relieved the truck was in the same location with no sign of the driver. The sun was a mirage, and my dry thoughts were dampened by further rain.

In retrospect, traveling from Athens to Rotterdam was instrumental in furthering my skills to overcome obstacles such as obtaining food, lodging, and transportation. The 1,800 miles covered by road—today a flight is around three and a half hours—became valuable lessons for future undertakings.

The trek to Rotterdam was demanding as described in a letter to my 10-year-old brother.

Dear Doug,

I made it to Rotterdam after two weeks. I arrived in Athens on July 31st and stayed for two days. I went to the Acropolis and Zeus's temple. I toured the city. There was not much to see in Athens, although it was a pleasant change from Israel. I hitchhiked on August 2nd, and reached Thessalonica, 500

kilometers away and close to Yugoslavia. It was along the sea.

The following day, I hitchhiked about 250 kilometers. The countryside gradually changed from low hills (1000' to 2000') with scattered trees to mountains, forests, and fields, with corn, wheat, pumpkins and other vegetables. There were rivers and beautiful valleys in Yugoslavia. Yugoslavia is the most liberal communist country. There is free enterprise, but signs of communism are evident, such as pictures of Stalin, red flags and stars, and unarmed soldiers.

The army service is compulsory for all 18-20-year-olds. In some parts of the country, you are prohibited to take photographs. It appears to be a hard life in the hills. I stayed in Belgrade for two days and caught a ride through the rest of Yugoslavia and the Austrian Alps (7000', which were magnificent) to Salzburg where I saw the Danube River and a castle. I don't remember now, but I believe it is called the headquarters of the King of Germany, and at one time, it was some sort of palace.

At this point, it started to rain, and it did not stop until I reached Rotterdam. Germany was a horrible place to hitchhike through. I stood in Munich (Bavaria) for 27.5 hours, and in Frankfurt for 8 hours. These were the places I had trouble hitchhiking. I left Germany after 4 long days. I saw the Rhine river in Bonn. My good luck was I rode with the Chief of Police of Aachen (a city in Germany) through the Dutch border and was not required to show my passport. He said, "This is a friend of mine" and into the Netherlands I went. It was quite lucky because I had no money.

I exhausted my money a few days before, but it lasted a long time. I only spent money on food, and I slept outside. You can trace my route on the map, along the coast of Greece, the center of Yugoslavia, directly north to Salzburg, Munich, Nuremberg, Wurzburg, Frankfurt, Bonn and the Netherlands.

I am living with a Dutch family (the Kooks) I hitchhiked with to Rotterdam until I find my own home or work. Mr. Kook's hobby is cooking Indonesian fare and he prepared a savory dinner. I expect to be earning ten dollars a day beginning tomorrow. First, I must get a work permit as there are many jobs here – good, easy jobs with respectable conditions. Without a permit, you get the opposite with the same pay. I am going to the embassy tomorrow to find out about getting a work permit. I hope to stay here until I earn enough money to travel further or else it is back home, and I do not want that to happen. I do not have an address yet, except for American Express, Rotterdam, Netherlands.

Your brother, Ron

At the central train station in Rotterdam, I was among fifty or more immigrants, mainly from Turkey and Morocco, as we awaited work as temporary laborers on the docks. The number of workers exceeded available jobs, which explained the pandemonium as the employers' vans arrived in the late afternoon. Each manager hired five or six men at a time. The willing workers crushed forward with arms flailing, yelling to capture the attention of the managers. Fortunately, I was chosen every day for work on the night shift.

My job involved cleaning the holds of freighters which was both dirty and dangerous. I and dozens of others wielded a scrub brush at the end of a six-foot pole as we precariously stood on loose planks of scaffolding. Without safety harnesses or railing, forty or fifty feet above the bottom of the cavernous steel hold, it was a less than ideal work environment. One misstep meant certain death into the oblivion of the hold.

With today's modern methods, I suspect cleaning the holds may be an easier, less hazardous process. When I was there, one sleepy miscalculation with the brush by me or a co-worker spelled death from the narrow platform. The job added new meaning to walking the plank.

The Netherlands' economy flowed with the trade of baking soda and chalk, and it was this residue I brushed up and down all night long. Without protective gear, we used an old cloth or piece of clothing to shield our mouths and noses. The white cloud of dust we created grew as the night progressed. We emerged at dawn through the cloud of dust like a posse of snowmen.

The advice from the other workers was to avoid cleaning out oil tankers. One slip and it was fifty feet into the remaining oil at the bottom of the hold. It is impossible to swim in oil, and this was not my preferred type of death. Thus, I cleaned the holds of the dry goods freighters since falling forty feet or more on to hard, cold steel is a nobler death than being fished out of fuel oil. It was a perilous and unhealthy job I endured for one week, earning money to travel to Amsterdam.

Ten days later, I was in Amsterdam, the renowned 'fun' capital of Europe, with its liberal laws of legalized prostitution and drugs. Some of the clubs served hash brownies. I was a twenty-one-year-old ready to embrace life in this city which was vibrant and tranquil at the same time.

The Dutch capital was an eclectic place, with widely varying food from its world-famous cheese to raw herring to Indonesian specialties. I indulged in many Indonesian restaurants, tasting beef rendang (beef cooked in coconut milk and spices), nasi goreng (fried rice) and satay (chicken barbequed on skewers and served with a peanut sauce). It was a world history lesson to comprehend the reason for the popularity of these establishments.

Indonesia was originally known as the Dutch East Indies. It was formed from the nationalized colonies of the Dutch East India Company, under the administration of the Dutch government in 1800, and the most valuable European colony under the Dutch Empire's rule. It contributed to Dutch global prominence in spice and cash crop trade in the 19th to early 20th centuries, and the term *Indonesia* referred to this geographical location after 1880.

Japan's World War II occupation dismantled much of the Dutch colonial state and economy, and following the Japanese surrender in August 1945, Indonesian nationalists declared independence which they fought to secure during the subsequent Indonesian National Revolution. The Netherlands formally recognized Indonesian sovereignty at the 1949 Dutch-Indonesian Table Conference. Today, there are 17,508 islands in the archipelago which has the world's fourth biggest population.

When I arrived in Amsterdam in 1970, twenty-five years after the end of World War II, the baby boomers had chosen a radical path compared to their parents. Exemplified by long hair, bell bottom pants, drugs, and a laissez-faire attitude, either love or hate was the general sentiment at the time. The news oftentimes reported hippies engaging in what appeared to be unseemly activities, and young people in general, were supposed to be feared, loathed, and punished for being different. The other side (the Establishment) chastised them and believed they led a bold and irresponsible way of life.

The aftermath of two world wars and the Depression affected life decisions for the succeeding generations. Adding to the Dutch social experience, the Vietnam War aside, the first American generation of the century to be free from world wars stepped into the spotlight. In a sense, the floodgates were opened, and long-haired hippies were free to travel the globe untethered, and many flocked to the Netherlands.

The reaction in other countries, including the Netherlands, was often fantastic, although small minds were, as always, sometimes fearful. Our elders pictured the end of the world while my interest and those of most of my colleagues was simply in touring the grandest destinations.

It was the 20th century, the planet was open for business, and airfares were affordable. It was a natural course of events to achieve balance from turmoil as times changed rapidly. The world's distribution of power was being shuffled, and the wheel of fortune was spinning, around and around. Where would it stop? The mood of the period was impatience—now or never. Part of this resulted from the tense cold war standoff that was a constant psychological backdrop. One nuclear bomb would ruin civilization.

Masses of people went to the airport to travel as an escape mechanism to cope with this ever-present threat; many came to Amsterdam. The passion for this city was contagious, and I caught Amsterdam fever. The invisible force of nature extended its hand welcoming everyone, and we converged from all around the world to participate in this dazzling extravaganza. The canal boats filled with tourists motored under the bridges, as people on bicycles and on foot crossed above. The prostitutes waited seductively behind their glass-enclosed display windows for their next customer.

The trams circled the city, transporting people hither and thither. The ringing of a bicycle bell proclaimed its presence to the unwary pedestrian: Keep walking, the show never stops. The crowds and entertainment are extraordinary. Breathe deeply, the air is crisp and fresh. The tempo is equivalent to a lively tango.

A stoned hippie after eating hash brownies with added chocolate goes home after a night at the Paradiso. He stops to converse with a woman scrubbing the sidewalk in front of her house in the early morning hours.

He had a groovy night, and to this day, many thousands of people still do. Paradiso is now in its fifth decade while sidewalk cleaning is now handled by the local government.

Housed in a converted former church building from the nineteenth century, Paradiso is in one of the main nightlife and tourism centers of the city. The primary concert hall has lofty ceilings and two balcony rings overlooking the stage area. Before 1965, it was the meeting hall for a liberal Dutch religious group and was abandoned until it was squatted by hippies in 1967. The church was converted into an entertainment and leisure club, and in 1968, it formally opened its doors for business as a publicly subsidized youth entertainment center.

In the 1970s, Paradiso was known as the world's best psychedelic music club. In recent years, the venue has featured an eclectic range of programming, which, besides rock and DJ'd club nights, includes lectures, plays, classical music, and crossover artists. Long associated with clouds of tobacco and hashish smoke, Paradiso banned smoking in its public areas (except for a small smoking room) in 2008 in accordance with a nationwide ban on smoking in public venues ...

A French backpacker in Rotterdam raves about the Paradiso. He is headed to Amsterdam and says this is the club for me. Now I understand, far out is an understatement.

On my first visit, each room has its own theme, and people sit around quietly, captivated by the sights and sounds. There is a recreational room on the first floor with food and drink.

The stoned hostess greets me with a smile. There are people buying and selling drugs, despite "no drug selling" signs conspicuously displayed.

The hostess breaks my reverie with a tap on my shoulder. Like an old-fashioned cigarette seller in the movies, she has a tray in front of her with a strap around her neck. She says something I can't comprehend and then repeats the phrase in English.

"I'm selling joints," she says. Her tray is full of ready-rolled joints.

"Thank you," she says as I put the change in my pocket.

In the next room, old Marx Brothers and Laurel and Hardy movies play on the large screens. An overhead projector in a black light room displays psychedelic shapes and colors onto the walls and ceiling.

At last, a lounge with several couches and chairs is filled with laughing and giggling hippies.

I fell in love with this city and its architecture, canals, boats, bicycles, trams, pedestrian-only paths, and parks. My long red hair and silk top hat contributed to the spectacle. They were key elements which became part of my business and personal success. It was the 'Summer of Love' Amsterdam-style.

TRACK TWELVE
JOHNNY CASH: GET RHYTHM

After a week of hard work in Rotterdam, I had a few weeks to enjoy myself in Amsterdam before the festival. With unbridled enthusiasm, I opted for the short train ride rather than hitchhiking for a change.

On my first day in Amsterdam, I was drawn to Club Paradiso for an evening of listening to music and smoking hash. I wasn't the only one with this idea, with fifty other would-be patrons eager to party. I was tightly funneled through the doorway as we neared the entrance. It was unnecessary to move; I was propelled forward by the sweaty bodies squashed around mine.

Once inside, the bone-crushing experience at the front door was well worth it. I visited the many themed rooms, soaking in the relaxed, casual atmosphere towards drugs and sex. I was eager to sample every aspect of the club's various rooms, and the lounge, snack bar, and movie room were my favorites.

In the lounge, huge joints were smoked, and pipes of hash were freely passed around. The stoned clubbers stared at the psychedelic posters on the wall as they laid on the comfortable pillows and couches, listening to the latest hits. A mini music festival best describes the scene, and everyone ambled from room to room, partaking in the festivities all night long.

The friendly zombies are happy being different although they are the same. Oh well, that's life in Zombie Land, coming soon to a neighborhood near you. I notice everyone has a little 'Z' emblem embroidered onto their clothing. It is easy to see the difference. In the distance, to my delight, there are many people with the letter 'H' instead. Who are these people, I wonder? "Hello, my name is Botron. Is the 'H' special?" Hal answers, "D-uh, of course. It is the best of all letters. We represent what others strive to become. You are obviously not an 'H'. Keep walking, Botron, until you find your letter in the alphabet soup of life."

The club closed, and too tired to go further, I slept on a bench in a nearby park. My elation in anticipating breakfast and another fun-filled day was overpowered by exhaustion as I snoozed for a few hours. I groggily awoke with the sunrise and immediately didn't feel the familiar bulge in my pants pocket. I was jolted to my feet with jaw agape as I felt an empty pocket. My wallet was gone. There was a pickpocket in line at the club. In a new city, without money or friends, this was an unexpected dilemma.

I roamed the streets of Amsterdam in a daze until Dam Square, a busy downtown tourist attraction. The focus of Dam Square is the World War II national monument, surrounded by the Royal Palace, museums, retail shops, and cafes. There are six steps leading to the monument, and sitting on the bottom step, I scrutinized the swarming crowds circling the square. A guitar player sang and strummed to my left, his guitar case open for coins, and a jewelry craftsman assembled necklaces to my right. These two small business entrepreneurs had a steady income, and I pondered my circumstances.

The jewelry craftsman created decorative wire pendants hung on a thin necklace, using pliers to bend and twist different abstract shapes. He had a constant stream of business, with a customer base of mainly women. This was naturally appealing to me as a future profession; however, an immediate profession was required.

My downtrodden eyes were directed toward the sidewalk. Shoes, shoes, and more shoes. In a flash, the light bulb moment occurred as my hungry stomach rumbled. Perfect timing. My elementary business plan was formulated as I thought, "This is my moment to shine! I will be a shoeshine boy in Dam Square, wearing a top hat!"

This jeweler became my original backer for the purchase of a shoeshine kit. I borrowed ten guilders (the equivalent of three U.S. dollars) to buy brushes and polish. My financial problems were solved in a matter of hours, as the business of shoe shining was brisk. Before I knew it, I had money in my pocket, and the loan was repaid.

"Hello, it's nice to meet you. Would you like a shoeshine? I'm working my way around the world one shoe at a time."

The customers came and went with shinier shoes, initiating their transformation. The pretty girl noticed the brilliance and met her new love. The salesman closed the important deal with added confidence after his shoeshine. The shattered, unemployed man with rejuvenated shoes found a job later that day. The tired tourist walked all day sightseeing and stopped to rest. The stories are countless. *Give Peace a Chance* played in the background.

"There is never a dull moment for those with shiny shoes," said the guru shoeshine boy.

"Your walk and talk will improve after you have your shoes shined here."

"Hello, young lady. Would you care to make a hippie happy?" I had all sorts of catch phrases for the passers-by who made their way through Dam Square.

I earned my living shining shoes, and the tranquil view of the river greeted my drowsy eyes each morning from the abandoned ferry station I now shared with seven other backpackers. It was a small one-story building with three concrete sides and one all-glass side facing the river. I picture multi-story condominiums there today, each worth millions of euros.

On my second day, it was opportune to meet Steven, a departing backpacker, who I replaced among the others who comfortably slept on the floor. He introduced me to the abandoned ferry station. The riverside abode lacked facilities, so I visited local youth hostels, filled with other tourists, to shower and shave.

My fellow riverside dwellers in the ferry station were an eclectic bunch of young men and women. Our nationalities initially consisted of one American man (me), an American woman, a Frenchman, a Dutchman, an Austrian woman, an Italian woman, and a German couple. The mix of nationalities changed frequently, as people came and went. The ferry station suited our purposes, and we were protected from the weather, cold, and all the unsavory nighttime aspects of a city. It was quiet and off the beaten path, yet two blocks to downtown and the central train station.

My breakfast of choice was espresso and sliced bread with cheese before 'the office'. The only shoeshine boy in Amsterdam was ready to change the world one shoe at a time. The vibrancy of the city was its main attraction. I was front and center in Dam Square with my long red hair and black top hat. As I shined shoes, I was photographed by tourists and journalists. Occasionally, I was given a guilder or two for the privilege of snapping my picture.

The eclectic nature of Dam Square was distinctive. Men, women, boys, and girls all congregated in the square. There were thousands of bystanders every day observing the hippie phenomenon, and this was a boost for my business. In a matter of days, young American tourists chose me as their tour guide for tasty food and fun places to visit. A stop on my tour was my favorite Indonesian restaurant where an entrée cost the equivalent of $2.00 for a generous portion. I now had two sources of income. The multitude of tourists, gawkers, workers, and ordinary pedestrians passed by, going to and fro. Next customer, please!

My group of friends were a variety of backpackers I met at Dam Square. Guy was my first friend. The revelation one day that he was broke surprised me. Guy revealed he was desperate and debated whether to return to the U.S. His tale began in the morning when he dejectedly sat in the square with his head placed upon his hand.

He was lost in a negative fog when he felt a gentle tap on his shoulder. He turned and gazed at a radiant young woman, an art student seeking a model to pose in her class; specifically, a nude one. Guy exclaimed he was an expert at removing his clothes. The center of attention, Guy sat naked on a stool for several hours surrounded by captivated art students. His future girlfriend, avidly sketching, was impressed by the preview.

"I made thirty guilders, man. I was saved. Now I'll never doubt myself again." I saw him a few times before he ventured elsewhere. Destiny was favorable to Guy.

The shoeshine business was nonstop entertainment in the square. I easily earned the equivalent of ten dollars a day in four hours—the equivalent of sixty-five dollars today. My work day began at eleven o'clock in the morning and ended at three o'clock in the afternoon. No reason to work all day.

For my own amusement, the hobby of studying shoes led to identifying personalities based on the condition of a person's shoes. The occasional female customer was the rare exception. There were caring people who advised me of the lowly position shining shoes represented. On the other hand, there were others who saw the brilliance of my job. No matter how many times I heard this, I chuckled at this common pun.

This business provided flexible hours, portability, and a large customer pool. I transformed a dirty job into a marvelous life. Other backpackers dealt with constraints based on their fixed budget, whereas I maintained a cash flow. This was my thought at the end of the day.

The Woodstock Music Festival film was released, and after hiding my shoeshine kit in a safe spot at the ferry station, it was a tram ride to the movie theater. Prior to the first frame, the flood of memories overwhelmed my senses with familiar sights and sounds. I relished reliving Woodstock.

One of the first to arrive, I purchased my ticket and located the best seat in the center of the theater which filled rapidly. It was obvious Woodstock was a well-known event internationally. An usher requested my ticket, and it appeared I was in the wrong seat because theater seating was reserved, unlike the 'sit anywhere you like' I was accustomed to.

As I envisioned having to move to a seat in a dark corner with an obstructed view, I handed my ticket to the usher. He glanced at it and then smiled before he switched the tickets and directed the other patron to his new seat. The reason for the usher to circumvent protocol was unknown. Perhaps he correctly guessed I was at Woodstock.

I savored every minute of the movie, reliving those spectacular days. In the middle of the movie, I was astonished to see my friend Lobster being interviewed as he exited one of the portable toilets with a pipe full of hash like a long-haired Sherlock Holmes. I wondered if he had seen the film yet.

"You want some?" Lobster asks the interviewer and cameraman individually with one of those 'happy' smiles as he offers the pipe. He is asked his opinion in regard to the facilities and, with a grin, answers it is "out of sight" and much better than the woods. I can agree with that. He asks the interviewer if this is for a movie and what it will be called.

"Port-O-San," he is told, to which he replies, "Far out."

I was glued to the screen as I remembered moment after moment of the fantastic time. Now I had the chance to enjoy Woodstock without the rain and mud and relive Jimi Hendrix—with his headband, white tasseled shirt, and blue velvet loon pants—playing his unique version of our national anthem. I was struck by the fact I was watching and listening in a foreign city. I was in Amsterdam, with the same flavor and core elements of Woodstock—music, hash, travelers, and hippies.

Lobster's knack of being at the right place at the right time was unwavering. A three-minute video of the Port-O-San worker emptying the toilets and Lobster's minute of fame landed on YouTube. At the time of this writing, this video has garnered tens of thousands of views.

The origin of Lobster's nickname was unknown. His reputation in Washington, DC was from his involvement in the mid-1960s music and dance TV show called *Wing Ding.* In the style of Dick Clark's *American Bandstand,* it featured some of the top acts at the time, plus emerging talent.

Lobster spoke of a performer dressed in cowboy gear who lip-synced to a new record on the show. At the end of the song, the host interviewed this singer and asked, "What state do you come from?" Based on his appearance, the host expected to hear Texas or Oklahoma. Instead, the singer replied, "I come from the state of Brooklyn." The host commented, "I guess they haven't gotten around to making that a state yet." The singer's name was Neil Diamond, and it was his first ever TV appearance.

One Saturday around midnight in late '68, Richie and I were stuck hitchhiking in a seedy section of Washington, DC when Lobster stopped his car and said, "Get in." We were somewhat surprised since the vehicle was packed with his entourage of seven, but he instructed us to lie prone across everyone else. This was when American cars were spacious, and we were relieved to have a ride. We piled onto the friendly laps of Lobster's girlfriends. Lobster to the rescue!

Several weeks before Woodstock, Lobster and I attended a Janis Joplin concert at the Merriweather Post Pavilion in Columbia, MD where we witnessed her amazing performance. As the audience streamed towards the exits at the show's end, Janis sang her first encore. At the end of the second, Janis waltzed to the edge of the stage, and after a brief conversation with Lobster, she offered him a swig from a bottle of Southern Comfort whiskey. He declined, and Janis resumed singing.

By the third encore, I had serious doubts of another since we were the last fifty fans in the audience, but the endless hollering from our group in front of the stage was successful. As Janis sang her fourth encore, I was impressed by her stamina, and questioned the obvious. With a grin, Lobster admitted, "I gave her, and everyone else in this group, a sugar cube."

Prior to the concert, he soaked a bag full of sugar cubes with a brown liquid which was 'MDA', similar to mescaline/amphetamine. This was the one and only time I witnessed four encores at a concert. The show must go on and on thanks to Lobster.

TRACK THIRTEEN
BUFFALO SPRINGFIELD:
FOR WHAT IT'S WORTH

As a daytime resident in Dam Square, my goal was earning the equivalent of ten dollars a day to cover my expenses and shoe polish. My daily shoe shining spot in the square was closest to pedestrian traffic. The consensus from a few locals was no one in the Netherlands shined shoes. Their rationale was shoe shining was perceived as a dirty and menial job.

With the earliest known ones dating from approximately 7,000 to 8,000 BC—found in Fort Rock Cave in the state of Oregon in 1938—shoes are the first form of improved transit, greatly extending the ability to traverse the world. The protection provided by shoes adds warmth and decreases the chance of cuts, infections, and more. Healthy feet, quite simply, ensure our survival. Our mobility and connection to the planet begin at our feet. The person with shoddy footwear is regarded as unobservant, lazy, or unmotivated—the components of a twelve-step program to mediocrity. Contrary to what some thought, for me, shoe shining was fun.

The world was my oyster and expecting the unexpected was normal for me. The world was also small. For instance, reuniting with my Bowie friends at Woodstock and another time bumping into a friend seven thousand miles from home at a B.B. King concert. Neither of us was aware of the other until the moment I sat down next to him. Similar incidents occurred in Amsterdam.

One afternoon in between customers, as the crowds strolled on the sidewalk past the square, a young man recognized me. He ran towards me and exclaimed, "Ron, it's Bruce!" He was my fourth-grade classmate, and we had not seen each other in thirteen years. My long red hair and top hat did not impede his powers of recognition. I was certain my appearance had changed from when I was eight years old. I was now several thousand miles away from our classroom.

It was uncanny to watch his quick calculation and his ability to recognize me. It was a pleasure to see Bruce again, as we were good friends in fourth grade until he moved to California. I don't have an explanation to life's unforeseen coincidences, other than the one my wise wife offered, "There are no coincidences."

Those quiet periods during my shoeshine day provided a daily opportunity to survey the legions of gawkers staring at the hippies on Dam Square. It was an endless parade of the curious, whose looks varied but whose thoughts seemed to be as one. We were mutual spectacles, sights not to be missed, ranging from the exotic to the endangered. This was ground zero for the hippie extravaganza, with activity everywhere as busloads of tourists poured into Dam Square. Shine your shoes, sir?

It's a small world when a polite gentleman walks towards me, but not for a shoeshine. He is an Israeli, happy to mention he saw me two months ago in Dizengoff Square in Tel Aviv. A fact of life is our presence never goes unnoticed. It is a two-way avenue of enlightenment, and the invisible forces set in motion happen every day. Here comes my friend Clarence.

He deserted the U.S. Navy to avoid Vietnam and tour the world. Clarence was a genuinely likeable character. He was a firm believer in marriage, to the extent he abandoned five wives in the previous two years. We chatted occasionally at Dam Square, and one afternoon he revealed his move to England. Clarence met a lovely English gal and intended to follow her. The last words he uttered as he waved goodbye were, "I'm going to marry her!" I can only guess how many times my pal repeated this phrase.

The neophyte tourists ask for information and request me to be their tour guide. They are correct in assuming the hippie with the long red hair and top hat knows the city. It is a natural progression from shoeshine boy to private tour guide. As I direct, "This way, please!" I am oblivious to the latest tempest slowly developing in Dam Square.

An anti-hippie crusade escalated in the media, portraying hippies as a menace to Dutch society. This elicited fear and loathing, and a warped bureaucratic process was under way. This influx of long-haired backpackers and youngsters was an unwelcome disruption to the status quo.

It is eerie how the fill-in-the-blank rhetoric and manufactured fear lead to violence. Jumping on this bandwagon, the tried and true formula for any aspiring politician is to exhibit the strength of a patriarch personified. The bureaucrats' belief is the populace demands their strong parental guidance and votes will soon follow.

In 2016, current Indonesian President Joko Widodo paid a working visit to the Netherlands, and this induced activists to demonstrate for the right of self-determination for South Moluccans and to protest human rights abuses in West Papua. The most controversial visit, however, was the first Indonesian state visit to the Netherlands, in 1970, by President Suharto. Perhaps he wasn't welcome when he was held responsible for the murder of hundreds and thousands of his fellow-countrymen only a few years earlier.

During his visit, Suharto was expected to place a wreath at the National Monument in Dam Square. In preparation, in late August 1970, the National Police were ordered to clear the square and demanded everyone leave or else. Their over-the-top encouragement for compliance caused major problems.

The violence erupted on Monday evening after hippies were commanded to vacate the National Monument. As youths battled with the police, Dam Square was a hub of activity, and my curiosity was piqued, which led to my downfall.

Drawn in by a sense of incredulity, the activity in the square was irresistible. I was among hundreds of spectators as less than a dozen protesters were sprayed by water cannons. It appeared the protest was ending soon due to the hundreds of well-equipped police with water cannons, personnel carriers, and vans.

In a short span of time, the chaos worsened, and mayhem reigned. Additional club-wielding policemen methodically attacked men, women, and children spectators, their only 'crime' being in the wrong place at the wrong time. Approximately twenty policemen charged our group, and everyone was clubbed to the ground. A vicious whack to my head was the price for being an innocent bystander, and my anger from previous injustices was unleashed.

The use of unnecessary violence invites natural retaliation. The frenzy escalated and became personal. Some clubbed spectators scurried away to quiet their racing hearts, while others grabbed cobblestones from the road to throw at police vans as pandemonium became the frightening norm. A lone policeman on the sidewalk panicked in the ensuing melee. I was sixty feet in front of him, in his direct line of fire, as he pulled his revolver from his holster. He fired repeatedly into the crowd, as we fled for our lives.

As the sounds of gunfire rang out, the man running beside me fell to the ground. I was impressed by his tactic to avoid being shot. The gunshots subsided within seconds, and his method of diving to the ground was not the brilliance I originally thought. He was shot in the back. The following day, the riot made banner headlines. The newspapers reported three people were shot during the riot; a senior citizen, and a student were shot thirty yards away from a photojournalist, who was the man running alongside me.

At that moment, Buzz, one of my acquaintances from Dam Square, grabbed my arm in disbelief. He was unable to comprehend the unprovoked violence and the fact of innocent people being shot. Buzz babbled about the bloody photojournalist somehow cutting himself on glass. My eighteen-year-old friend was in shock after witnessing these horrific incidents. I was of little assistance in my attempt to ease his troubled mind. He was incapable of believing the circumstances, and it was the last time I saw Buzz.

The ferry station was my sanctuary after the hysteria at the square. The consequence of the riot for me was a terrible headache and a lump on my head from the clubbing. In the morning, my ferry station friends conversed as they read the daily newspaper. They turned the newspaper toward me, and there I was on the front page throwing a cobblestone and yelling at police to stop attacking innocent bystanders. I was as stunned as my friends. Their advice was to leave town immediately. With a few guilders in my pocket, I was on the road within an hour.

With the Isle of Wight music festival as my destination, I hitchhiked to the port city of Ostend, Belgium. The nine-hour ferry ride to Dover was smooth, and the stress from the last few days abated. I couldn't wait to attend this epic event and to see Jimi Hendrix. This euphoria was short-lived when at immigration in England I was refused entry for insufficient funds. After paying for the ferry fare, the single Dutch penny in my pocket brought me to a screeching halt.

Here I was in a waiting room praying for a miracle among other rejected entrants, many of them festival bound. We were a dozen or more detainees in limbo, and in front of me was a girl from Brussels named Caroline. She and I brainstormed different ways to clear immigration. After the officials spoke with her a second time, she rushed back with her news.

"They contacted my friend in England," she exclaimed, "I was granted entry!"

In my distracted mind, I only heard snippets of her voice:

"I'm a Trotsky ... and my apartment ... Ron, are you are listening?"

Slow realization dawned of her being my savior when she repeated what she'd said.

"Ron, you can stay in my apartment in Brussels for a few days. Simply put the key in the mailbox when you leave."

Caroline scribbled her address on a piece of paper and mentioned there was food in the pantry. I was rendered speechless when she added she had a job contact in Luxembourg, her former boyfriend Nicholas, the son of a NATO general.

The ferry company was obligated to return me at no charge to the originating country once I was refused entry. It was problematic to hitchhike from Ostend to Brussels. My impression of Belgium was hippies were unwelcome as evidenced by the stares and unfriendly gestures from locals and many yelled "Go back to Amsterdam" in English.

Caroline's apartment was my refuge for the weekend before hitchhiking to Luxembourg. Five days later, with Caroline's letter of introduction in hand, I knocked on the door of a large, stately home in Luxembourg answered by a butler. Nicholas was called, and after reading the letter, he suggested I join him for dinner and meet his parents. This culture clash between the hippie and the general was an unexpected dynamic in my job search.

As the general, his wife, and son studied the hippie in their midst, it was an awkward, yet delicious meal in the formal dining room. In the center of this huge room was a heavy wood table with ornately hand-carved pedestal legs, surrounded by fourteen chairs. Nicholas, his mother, and father sat at one end of the table. My chair was at the head of the table on the opposing end facing the general, the vast empty table between us. This was the most outlandish job interview of my life.

As servants brought our courses, my story was told as the general listened. He was unsympathetic, and his advice was to work and attend university in the U.S. He assured me all my problems would be solved. Excellent advice for someone other than me. Nicholas's one-to-one advice after dinner was to backtrack to Amsterdam. He generously paid my fare to Amsterdam. For a stranger who appeared out of nowhere on his doorstep, Nicholas rose above and beyond to fulfill a request from an ex-girlfriend. Two magnanimous people who came to my aid.

A two-hour drive by car from Brussels to Luxembourg had been a difficult two-day hitchhike without food or money. This was the reason for my reluctant decision to rejoin my ferry station roommates. My nerves were on edge when I spoke with my roommates to hear what happened after my departure. Klaus graphically described the post-shooting riots which lasted three days. The second day was the worse, when over one hundred Marines from bases outside Amsterdam, acted, it was reported, without orders, and savagely attacked hippies and backpackers in the square and environs. There were injuries to many innocent bystanders. Now the media and the politicians changed their spin, and Premier Piet de Jong ordered an investigation into the controversial action by the Marines.

On the third night, a force of three hundred and fifty policemen was dispatched to prevent young people from entering Dam Square, and several protesters were reported to have hurled smoke and gasoline bombs. Nine people, including three policemen, were injured, and thirteen demonstrators were arrested.

Calm was restored after the third night and the post-disturbance inquiries concluded the riots were not started by "international visitors," but by groups of local youths and troublemakers. To this day, there is still controversy surrounding the Marines viciously assaulting hippies—both male and female—and the violence was not confined to Dam Square; others were also attacked and seriously injured in various downtown locations.

I resumed my shoeshine business and daily routine for three weeks until one morning before me were two pairs of boots shining like mirrors. They belonged to two policemen in front of me. One had a stern expression on his face, and the other looked elated as if he won a grand prize.

A lone Dutchman had recognized me from the three-week-old newspaper photo and immediately informed the authorities. The police swooped in from all directions as I was escorted to their van. I managed a hurried goodbye to my jeweler friend and abandoned my shoeshine kit.

Huis van Bewaring, a detention center near downtown Amsterdam, was my new home. In a back room, I was stripped naked and beaten by eight policemen. This practice was a common occurrence after an arrest. Two black eyes, a split lip, and multiple other bruises later, I was placed in a cell for the next thirty days. Although sparse, it had a bed, chair, table, and radio. Meals were served in the cell, and the food was surprisingly appetizing.

The other inmates were all eighteen to twenty-one-year-olds, except for the Dutch equivalent of Charles Manson, who was serving a life sentence. I did not know his exact age, but he was arrested in the 1920s. He resembled the Birdman of Alcatraz.

In the afternoons, we were permitted to wander the tiers and visit fellow inmates which were of various nationalities. Along with other Americans, there were Dutch, British, and French to name a few. I was the last person arrested from the riot. To occupy my time, I volunteered to assemble clothespins, an activity providing a small distraction. Incarceration was a difficult adjustment compared to my pre-riot carefree existence.

As the days passed, it became the worst of times as the mental hammer came crashing down. My positive outlook was on hold as I thought of my Danish girlfriend, who drew a map to her house. Would I ever see her again? Furthermore, a new sense of sadness was exacerbated by the death of Jimi Hendrix. I was fortunate to be at Woodstock for his epic performance. Sixteen days later, the death of Janis Joplin was announced. I attended many of her concerts, and she is one of my favorite singers. The world lost two major music icons of the era, and my sadness increased as if I lost two more close friends.

My court appearance for the charge of disturbing the peace was scheduled during my third week in detention. I was sentenced to thirty days with time served; in addition, my obligation was to reimburse Pan American Airways for the flight. I was deported to New York City just in time for Halloween. It was not a treat for me. This was now the second time in two years I missed my goal of circling the world through Europe and on to Asia and the Pacific. Another piece of my heart was broken.

It was a true Monopoly board game experience when I had to leave Amsterdam. Go directly to jail, and do not collect $200. In the rear of a 747 on a KLM flight from Amsterdam to JFK airport, I dug deep to make sense of the past few months. What was the message? What was the lesson? The rapid fire of calamities in the last few years left its indelible mark on my psyche. I was devastated and crushed with despair. These uncommon circumstances became far too common for me.

After clearing Immigration for re-admission into the U.S., I was lost in a fog, in search of a brief respite from my soap opera life. Flushing Meadow Park (site of the 1964 World's Fair near JFK airport) was where I joined other hippies to smoke pot. Unbeknownst to me, the park was a popular spot for young hippies to party away from nosy neighbors. As we smoked and blabbed, it became evident they were intrigued by my reports on Amsterdam. I was ignorant of this fact until that moment. What others perceived as extraordinary was the daily news for me. My recent dance with adversity coupled with a new acceptance of this unexpected detour slowly simmered. I concluded to take a vacation from my vacation for now.

> *Who am I in the grand scheme? The iceberg floats in the ocean, just a small portion visible above the surface. It is a mesmerizing sight as it glistens in the sunlight, the many facets of the ice like unpolished gems. No matter which direction it moves, the iceberg shines as it glides through the water. This wandering behemoth, lost in the vast ocean, contentedly dreams of familiar faces. Adrift, it is a seafaring beacon for aimless wanderers.*

TRACK FOURTEEN
THE MOODY BLUES: QUESTION

The U.S. drug culture in late 1970 was in stark contrast to the liberal Netherlands, with abundant availability of drugs across the country. The experimentation with illegal drugs was rising in the U.S. despite a national police crackdown to stop the flow. Subsequently, crime rates crept higher.

While drugs were illegal, weapons, especially advanced weapons, were not, and in October, the U.S. Foreign Office announced the renewal of arms sales to Pakistan. Meanwhile, the Vietnam War escalated, and in Paris, a Communist delegation rejected U.S. President Richard Nixon's peace proposal, stating it was "a maneuver to deceive world opinion." Nixon's response was to withdraw 40,000 additional U.S. troops before Christmas.

In November, the U.S. handed control of the air base in the Mekong Delta to South Vietnam, and U.S. Military Assistance Command reported the lowest weekly American soldier death toll in five years. Twenty-four young men lost their lives that week, and another 431 soldiers were reported wounded.

The winners in the last quarter of 1970 included the Baltimore Orioles baseball team, who defeated the Cincinnati Reds 9-3 in game five of the World Series, to win the series four games to one for their 2nd World

Championship. Others with reason to celebrate were the Democrats who swept to victory in the U.S. Congressional mid-term elections. Jimmy Carter was elected as Governor of Georgia, and George Wallace was elected as Governor of Alabama. The Republicans also celebrated as Ronald Reagan was re-elected as Governor of California.

Also, in November, the Supreme Court voted 6-3 to *not* hear a case by the state of Massachusetts questioning the constitutionality of a state law granting Massachusetts residents the right to refuse military service in an undeclared war. Meanwhile, Richard Nixon requested $155 million in supplemental aid from the U.S. Congress for the Cambodian government, $85 million of which was for military assistance to prevent the overthrow of Premier Lon Nol's regime by the Khmer Rouge and North Vietnam.

Back home in Bowie, I was recovering from the shock of being deported and distracted myself by listening to record albums and the radio. I was reminded of Lobster when a local radio station DJ announced Neil Diamond's first number one hit *Cracklin' Rosie*; I later noticed on TV his cowboy outfit was discarded. In late December for a period of three weeks, George Harrison was in the number one spot with *My Sweet Lord,* a song he later agreed he'd "subconsciously plagiarized" from a 1963 song called *He's So Fine* by The Chiffons which lasted less than two minutes. Both songs were similar.

I was demoralized to have my latest exploits to circumnavigate the world redirected twice as my friends rallied to elevate my spirits. Richie, from our grocery shopping spree in Florida, his girlfriend Pam, and I were invited to a harvest moon party on the outskirts of Bowie.

A dozen or so of our friends gathered in a quiet, secluded spot near the railroad tracks. This was the perfect place for an outdoor party without disturbing the neighbors. We partied, drank beer, and smoked pot. As the night progressed, Richie and I reflected on our fun escapades in Orlando.

"Hey Ron, it's damn boring in Bowie," Richie stated, rising to his feet. "Wouldn't it be great to go to Orlando again?"

"I agree!" I replied with a grin; this was an excellent idea for another trip. "Let's leave tomorrow?"

My question was answered by a freight train which rumbled down the tracks behind us and, seizing the opportunity, Richie dashed to run alongside. Impatient Richie wasn't one for delay, and time was of the essence.

A speedier runner than me, Richie was fifty feet ahead when I ceased running because the train traveled faster than I expected. The deafening noise of the train drowned my yells as my calls to wait went unheeded. In a split second, Richie lost his footing. I was aghast as the protruding iron ladder on the side of the boxcar struck Richie in the head with such ferocity he was flung sideways before landing on the ground ten feet from the tracks.

In stunned silence, I was buried under an avalanche of confusion. Pam was beside Richie, screaming uncontrollably as she knelt over his motionless body. All our friends immediately sensed something catastrophic occurred. Andy flew into his car toward the nearest public phone to call for an ambulance.

Richie was taken to the hospital, and in our disoriented state, we stumbled into cars to follow. We sought to calm ourselves during the drive by recalling Richie's previous instances of good luck, endeavoring to convince each other of his recovery. Richie will have an interesting story relating to our party by the railroad tracks, we told ourselves.

This was not the case. At the hospital, we were given the tragic news of Richie's death by the doctors. I once more faced the fragility of life. I'd also recently lost a friend in Vietnam, and now another one was added to the list, in the cruelest of circumstances. Richie was barely nineteen years old; a brief lapse of judgment had ended his life.

His death was reported in the local newspaper, and the article cemented the fact of losing another friend. The outpouring of grief on the day of his funeral was heartbreaking and surreal. This was the second time in two years I had witnessed the death of a close friend. One miscalculation caused instant death, a grim reminder that life is fickle and fleeting.

Richie's accident further reinforced my belief to treasure every moment. The notion I controlled my life was shattered. It was nothing other than some grand illusion. The traditional values were irrelevant now; Bowie was an alien world, and I yearned to be somewhere else.

Hailed initially as a significant success, William Levitt's overnight creation of a new community in Bowie developed major side effects. The influx of thousands of residents with no attachment to the town was an unusual occurrence. It was a magnet because of abundant job opportunities and inexpensive housing. Most residents were not from the area, and as they flooded in from elsewhere, a mini melting pot was created in what was a small Maryland town.

The evolution of Bowie was constructed speedily and methodically in an ongoing 'assembly line' which lasted for decades. The construction was nonstop as, on average, fifty to eighty houses were completed per day until ten thousand homes were added to the haphazard growth. The additional infrastructure of the town, including schools, banks, shopping centers, churches, libraries, and other essentials were built over a ten-year period. Bowie was in its initial stages of growing pains.

The original tobacco farms surrounding Bowie disappeared as rows upon rows of tract houses were erected, destined to be called 'home' by families with no allegiance to anything beyond their own four walls. My family descended into the crucible called Belair in Bowie as it bubbled and churned to produce a new environment. My original belief was that Bowie was a typical suburban town like every other town in the country, yet having traveled to other established towns, I soon recognized Bowie's different attributes.

Opportunities arose to meet new friends from other parts of the U.S. and the world. As we shared our life stories, it became evident my belief of Bowie being typical was inaccurate. My newfound friends also concluded Bowie wasn't a true representation of suburban life in the U.S. I considered the effects of the sudden birth and growth cycle of a lone town on its residents compared with an older, mature town. Is there a difference?

In early November after Richie's accident, Kurt—sightseer of cornfields—called and suggested a trip to New York City with our friend Greg. The purpose was to visit his Bowie friend Della, now living in Manhattan, and to buy some LSD. His efforts to provide a distraction fit the bill.

The next morning, the three of us hitchhiked from Bowie to New York. We rode with a driver of a moving van headed to New York City after his delivery in Aberdeen, MD. We earned seven dollars each for approximately three hours of labor offloading furniture and household possessions. We became movers for the afternoon; however, our arrival into the city was delayed until 11:00 p.m.

New York City in the 1970s was not the gentrified metropolis of today. Now lined with luxury apartments, The Bowery, nicknamed Skid Row, was a seedy neighborhood which housed illicit activities, and was a haven for drug dealers, prostitutes, and winos. Decades of industrial decline and economic stagnation caused a dramatic downturn for America's largest city while depopulation and arson led to abandoned blocks dotting the landscape.

Crime and financial crises became the dominant themes of the decade. From 1969 to 1974, New York lost 500,000 manufacturing jobs, which resulted in over one million households becoming dependent on welfare by 1975. In a similar span, rapes and burglaries tripled, while car thefts and felony assaults doubled. Murders grew from 681 to 1,690 per year.

This was the atmosphere during our visit to the Bowery, where it was unnervingly quiet in the city as we walked to Della's. With newfound earnings in our wallets, I had four hundred additional dollars for expenses in my pants pocket. The three of us were headed to Della's as darkness descended upon us when a booming voice suddenly emanated from the nearby shrubbery along the sidewalk.

"Hey guys, where are you going? I'm a policeman. This is a dangerous area, go home."

This was the one and only time I spoke to a policeman stationed in shrubbery. The level of danger was off the charts. Kurt and Greg were lost in locating the apartment while I was their impatient friend with urgency to be indoors. Despite the policeman's warning, Kurt and Greg were blissfully unaware we were sitting ducks in the arcade of stupidity. Our timing was far from perfect when we arrived at Della's apartment at 11:30 p.m. ... only to discover she was not at home.

On the sidewalk outside her apartment building, two desperados emerged in a matter of minutes. One of them robbed Kurt and Greg of their day's earnings. I was brusquely addressed by the other hoodlum whose weapon of choice was a knife. It was a robbery.

"Give me your wallet," he demanded, which I nervously handed to him.

The seven dollars I earned was a small loss; however, this was not the end of our interaction. He was a seasoned criminal and menacingly pointed to each of my pockets with his knife, demanding to see the contents. All of them were empty, except for the four hundred dollars under my handkerchief. I calmly removed my dirty handkerchief and waved it in front of his face.

At this point, his partner called for him to skedaddle. The hoodlum stuck his knife tip one inch from my nose and barked, "If I find out you have more money, I'll kill you."

In the next few minutes, we discussed what happened, and I asked Kurt and Greg why they were overly cooperative with two-to-one odds versus the robber. Kurt said he wielded a gun, thereby negating any odds in their favor. Della arrived within a few minutes, and the reason proffered for her delay was because she bought heroin; this clarified everything. In the future, let's hope my two clueless friends will avoid a den of junkies, desperate to pay for their next fix.

Our morning wake-up call was a rock thrown through the window of Della's first-floor apartment; we guessed it was a message for Della to pay a debt. I shoved Kurt and said, "Let's get out of here." Nonplussed, Della arranged for Kurt to buy LSD from her friend Pinky at nearby St. Mark's Place, a street in lower Manhattan full of shops frequented by hippies and drug dealers. I lent Kurt money for his purchase, relieved the end of this fiasco was drawing near.

We rode the Greyhound bus home and, for once, I was anxious to leave Manhattan. The vacation I envisioned was postponed for another time with different friends. I reflected on my situation and my search for an answer during the bus ride. My inability to calm the madness during the past few years compounded the insanity. I was oblivious to my downward spiral, highlighted by recent dramatic events including the robbery in Manhattan. Questions swirled in my mind.

The wild thoughts of a twenty-one-year-old percolated. With limited opportunities, I asked for advice, and the consensus was to work. The counsel I received was of little help. I was flooded by a tsunami of memories cascading across my mind as I celebrated New Year's Eve 1971. My resolution was to change direction, both literally and metaphorically.

My small glimmer of an idea may manifest into something concrete. In the past, both my good and bad choices ended dismally. The simple solution was to recover from my traumas before embarking on a career. I discerned it was a wise choice to pursue later. Then I reflected on the good times shared with new acquaintances during my last two travel attempts to circle the world and yearned for more.

The rapid succession of each catastrophe had allowed little time for recovery. I was the proverbial pinball pushed erratically from bumper to bumper. The invisible forces had the last word. It was not easy, but my resolution was for more fun. The eureka moment materialized: I would reverse direction and travel westbound around the world.

> *Life would be simple with traffic lights and predetermined routes. We have that, I heard ... be born, mature, and die. This is the process. What happens when life mushrooms and veers off course? It creates questions until thoughts equal pain. This breeds a desire to live fully. What is the formula? Life is a trip.*
>
> *The ocean and the tides are eternal forces on our planet. That's the answer!*

TRACK FIFTEEN
THE BEATLES: BLACKBIRD

The bell clangs as I enter the ring and confront the baggage. Its heaviness looms in the air. It is an albatross, impossible to avoid. I lunge forward onto the bag, and as we wrestle, I am winning. I am the victor. Freedom! Slowly, it overpowers and pins my body firmly onto the mat. The weight of the bag presses on my chest, and I am unable to breathe, my arms flailing. Darkness descends like an old movie where the image fades to a dot.

I awoke and saw my backpack on the floor. Onward! I grabbed the pack and sprinted out the door. Impatience ruled the night. With a few dollars and without a map, my objective was to finish circling the world.

"Go west, young man," Horace Greeley once said, and that is the way to go. I will go west to the ocean ... which is there to be crossed. As Phineas Fogg remembered the day he launched his around the world journey, so did I. I prayed for success on my first westward bound route.

On February 8th, 1971, at 8:00 p.m., the same time as I hitchhiked on the side of the dark Maryland highway, Bob Dylan's hour-long documentary film, *Eat the Document*, premiered at New York City's Academy of Music. I don't know what it was like in New York, but it was a cold night, with a few cars on the road. The prospects for my trip were rapidly collapsing.

The sensible way to travel is to purchase an around the world airline ticket and have sufficient funds to stay at youth hostels. It was an attractive and tempting option, yet one that did not match my impatience. This involved working for a year and risking the possibility of a permanent attachment to the area. A huge endeavor was the next step to regain stability in my life. I opted to seize the moment, and this decision ignored common sense.

The minutes slowly added doubt to this first leg of my journey. The initial step into the abyss had been taken, and my fate blew in the cold wind. Fear surfaced, I was naked and exposed to the extremes of life. The daily newspaper headlines reported the dangers of being a speck and a blur on the highway at night. Emblazoned in huge letters to frighten future hitchhikers from becoming naively adventurous, the headline in the morning will read "**Dead Hippie Found Frozen on Road**." On this damp and bone-chilling night, I wished one person would stop for this amateur world traveler.

Thirty minutes later, the cavalry came to the rescue in the shape of a 1964 Chevrolet Impala. The visions of my comfortable apartment vanished, and as excitement coursed through my body, my smile circled the globe. The driver said he was headed to West Virginia. I loved that first word. As I jumped into the car, a frozen hitchhiker statistic on the side of the highway was averted as heat from the vents warmed my feet and beyond.

The start of the journey was now official, and alpine horns trumpeted. I was intoxicated by the thoughts of seeing foreign lands, cultures, and cuisines. The stars winked, and the wind howled in agreement. In the middle of the night, on the shoulder of a West Virginia road, I was let off and began to hitchhike with resolve.

In the darkness of the night, the moon was absent, and I was barely visible on the side of the road. Breathe deeply. Think. Do I press on regardless of the outcome? The doubt was short, and the answer was simple. Adventure was further down the highway, beyond the memories. Beginners luck surfaced with another ride to Terre Haute, Indiana. This success in the middle of the night erased my doubts.

On the outskirts of Terre Haute, it was a cold, windy winter's morning on a two-lane country road lined with desolate cornfields. The prominent Terre Haute welcome sign cast a shadow as I shivered. In the distance, smoke billowed from a farmhouse chimney, and I imagined a warm fireplace, and the farmer's wife preparing breakfast. I smelled the dark, black coffee brewing, the cast iron frying pan cooking eggs, and bacon crackling, with bubbling aromas emanating up the chimney.

"Let's eat breakfast," my stomach begged.

The desolate road had nary a car or pedestrian in either direction. The headline will now read, "**Frozen Hungry Hippie Found Dead**." To stay warm, I trotted along the road in search of a store when the next ride stopped. **"Hippie Happily Leaves Terre Haute"** is the updated headline. As I said goodbye to this town, named 'High Land' in French by explorers in the early 18th century, I will visit another time.

As the car's heater warmed my body, the driver was quiet, uninterested in my destination of "around the world." Those moments of semi-isolation were for brief reflection. The simple decision upon a fork in the road on a cold winter's day was a defining one. Go west, young man, was my fate. I asked where we were, and the answer was "near Illinois." Good enough for me. I was on course in a westerly direction. The driver stopped for gasoline, and this was my chance to have a snack before I ventured further. "Thanks for the ride," I said.

My confidence was building, and with a full stomach, I surveyed the highway, as many cars, trucks, and motorcycles passed at varying speeds. This was an improvement. My probability of hitchhiking across the U.S. in the middle of winter increased significantly until the endless drone of tires pounding the highway became tiresome. I chuckled at the root form and true visual of the word "tiresome."

The sounds of the highway became a monotonous drone. With my steady progress, I fantasized a warm and toasty locale somewhere in California within a week. The wind roared across the plains as I stood by the entrance ramp to the expressway. An airplane flew through drifting clouds in the sunny sky. I suspected the passengers on board were warm, landing at their destination in a few hours. Their schedules safe and predictable in contrast to mine.

Another vehicle approached, and I extended my thumb once more. Success! Barry and Wendy, a friendly newlywed couple, stopped and said, "We are headed to Joplin, Missouri." My slow and less than smart outset gained momentum when they said it was 500 miles ... due West.

These newlyweds were beginning their lives together, full of love, and unrestrained joy, and it was a treat to join them on this part of their trip. It was early evening when we neared their home. Wendy suggested not to hitchhike near this location at night because it was dangerous. I didn't have a choice with only a few dollars. They offered to pay for my overnight lodging at the motel owned by a friend of Wendy's father.

"Don't want no hippies in here," he informed us to which Wendy replied, "My daddy won't be happy with you when I tell him." I guessed he was a local bigwig.

The motel owner refused to budge, and to my utter surprise, Wendy said, "You'll stay with us at my parents' house." I was saved from the freezing temperatures by another act of human kindness. As I dreamt 24 hours earlier, Wendy's mother skillfully prepared a scrumptious breakfast of eggs, bacon, grits, and toast before Wendy and Barry drove me to the highway the next morning.

From the expressway ramp, I waved goodbye to these two newlyweds and wished them a happy life. Farm after farm dotted the brown, barren landscape along the highway. It was a colder day than the day before as the wind persistently pounded my back. The first car stopped, and the driver said, "I'm going to Topeka, Kansas," 200 miles northwest. "Sounds great," I said as I hopped in.

It was smooth sailing until somewhere near Lawrence, KS. A storm intensified into a blizzard, screaming across the plains. It was the first time I had witnessed snow falling horizontally like millions of flying strands of spaghetti. Most likely it was the onset of my hunger pangs which elicited this vision.

The strength of the wind created long, straight, white lines of snow across our path and, combined with the ever-growing snowdrifts, increased my respect for the perilous side of Mother Nature. He drove cautiously, unsure if the side of the road or the tail end of the car in front of us would be our next stop. Cars and trucks were in a slow race to the next town, the drivers hoping to avoid the worst of the storm as the snow accumulated relentlessly on the highway.

A road sign emerged out of the gloom and declared, "Topeka 30 miles." I fancied the safety of a warm, cozy house with my legs stretched on an ottoman while my bare feet tingled from the warmth of a blazing log fire. It was an enticing image, but one far from reality.

Luckily, Topeka, the halfway point across the country for me, greeted us without incident. My ride ended in front of a convenience store as the owner prepared to close. In eight inches of snow, raging, angry ice crystals pelted my body. In a trance, as I was captivated by the blizzard, a voice sprang out of the ether.

"Are you looking for a place to stay?" asked the voice, which belonged to someone my age. He introduced himself as Richard Nixon. In my bewilderment, I asked myself is it possible to hallucinate in a blizzard?

"Yes, I sure am!" I said with a sigh of relief.

"No, I'm not the President, but I'm having a blizzard party with some college buddies. If you don't mind, you can sleep on the floor."

"Works for me," I replied and off we went.

Appropriately, his comfortable home resembled a miniature White House. Richard, his friends, and I drank, talked, and drank some more as they discussed the beauty of Kansas. With the mention of my prior and intended travels, Richard was slightly envious and voiced his desire to visit the ocean someday for the first time. His ambition was to become an attorney, an ambition as unwavering as mine to tour the world. I discovered a new paradise in Kansas and, along with Terre Haute, someday I'll tour the Midwest.

The blizzard raged until the early hours of the morning. Babies were born in cars buried in snowdrifts. Vehicles were trapped on the side of the road, and people froze. We awoke to brilliant sunshine, glistening snow, and not a single puff of wind. Abandoned cars were dug out as roads were plowed. Topeka was vibrant with activity when I revisited the convenience store for breakfast. A hot cup of coffee and a donut is a fantastic way to start the day's journey, especially when you meet someone named Gus.

"Where did you find shelter last night?" I asked as we sat in front of the shop window and observed the activity outside.

"I got the last room in the motel next door," he replied before he extended his hand and introduced himself. He was young with short hair.

"Are you in the Army?" I asked as we shook hands.

"Yes, I'm driving to San Francisco. The U.S. Army is giving me an all-expenses-paid vacation to Vietnam." His sense of humor was refreshing.

I answered his questions regarding my plans, and Gus invited me to ride with him. I thanked fate or whatever led me to that fork in the road, and the ride north. In a few days, I bid goodbye to winter and hello to my 1,800-mile ride west.

Gus and I cruised past mile after mile of abandoned cars buried in snow. The aftermath of the blizzard left stranded vehicles of all shapes and sizes buried along the highway for at least thirty miles. We eventually left the snow and were greeted by better weather conditions further west.

"After Salina, we have a choice," advised Gus, who was ahead of schedule for his deployment. "We can either drive via Salt Lake City and Reno or take a little detour south to Las Vegas and then back up. So, what do you think, Ron?"

"Well, I …"

"Yep! We're going to Vegas!" he pronounced, and I grinned.

The southerly route to bypass another blizzard was also my choice. We avoided the route of the ill-fated Donner Party wagon train whose members, in the winter of 1846-47, resorted to cannibalism to survive.

In 1971, Las Vegas was different from the bustling city it is today with a population close to 126,000 compared to the 648,000 who live there now. Before we arrived in the heart of the city around 1:00 a.m., we bypassed stretches of undeveloped land which are now covered with monster-sized office buildings, high rise apartments, hotels, and casinos.

Gus chose to gamble in the Golden Nugget casino based on its reputation as the best casino in the city and its central location in downtown Las Vegas. Originally built in 1946, today it is one of the oldest casinos in the city. Our rendezvous was agreed upon for 10:30 a.m. in front of the Golden Nugget to continue our drive, and Gus disappeared inside to play craps.

Inexpensive buffets were offered for $1.99, including free drinks. My best option for the evening was to play blackjack at $2.00 per hand. With $12.00 in my pocket, I was a player. Without a hotel room, my desire was to sleep with Lady Luck.

The cards were dealt, and I won a few hands and lost a few. This roller coaster cycle of winning and losing lasted several hours. My rudimentary knowledge was enough for me to play on and off all night until 5:00 a.m. when my winnings totaled $40.00. I quit while I was ahead and heartily consumed the $1.99 breakfast buffet followed by city sightseeing before our rendezvous.

Las Vegas to Reno is a seven-hour ride along the edge of Death Valley and the Inyo National Forest. As we drove under the Reno Arch, the sign welcomed us proclaiming 'The Biggest Little City in the World'. Gus and I were ready for the biggest little lunch in the world at a small burger stand. In gambling country, the place was large enough for six slot machines on the outer wall with six stools along the counter. As Gus nursed a coffee at the counter, I was bored and played the slot machines.

The routine was a few customers played the slot machines while they waited for their orders. The clerk yelled, "Order up for #27" and the customer vacated the slot machine for his burger and fries. With five nickels in my pocket, I played three nickels in the abandoned machine and lost. The fourth nickel hit a jackpot! Oh, nothing compares to a little easy money.

The clerk yelled, "Order ready for #28." I played the slot machine left by diner #28. The wheels spun, and another jackpot banged and clanged into the tray. I was astounded. Two jackpots in a row! This was incredible. The clerk yelled, "Order ready for #29."

Diner #29 at the far-right slot machine collected his order, and I sauntered to his vacated machine. I inserted a nickel into the slot and pulled the handle. Nothing. I dropped in one more and heard the all-too-familiar sound of nickels falling into the tray for another jackpot as the clerk yelled, "Order ready for #30." My order of burger and fries.

I shared my winnings with Gus, and we devoured our burgers before the final leg of our ride. I have played a lot of slot machines since then and have yet to win another jackpot. Never to meet again, I hope Gus had a safe tour in Vietnam. We parted near San Francisco, where I traveled south. Although it is more convenient to visit major cities, I avoided San Francisco and Los Angeles on this leg. San Francisco was the epicenter of the counterculture during this period; however, smaller towns were my choice. I headed towards Monterey.

> *Reflections are as granular as grains of sand. I can't explain the unfathomable. I'll defer to the experts.*

> *I am the sandman. I drive a truck to and fro. I transport sand from the desert and deliver the sand to the seashore. The redistributed sand on the beach is a resort area. The desert sands are less appealing, except to a wandering Bedouin. The Bedouin drinks mint tea, lounging in his tent to avoid the sun among the sands.*

> *The beachgoers dance and prance in the sand while the sun shines. The beachgoers worship the sand, as they build sandcastles and sip pina coladas. The jolly children, carefree on the shore, shriek with gusto before dashing into the sea.*

> *The Bedouin sits on his carpet with his cup of tea. The desert is vast and unforgiving. The Bedouin allows the wind to be his guide, unlike the beachgoers who await their orders from above. The sands of time pass. It is too late for the beachgoers to see the desert. The sandman drives to and fro, beaming all the way.*

TRACK SIXTEEN

JEFFERSON AIRPLANE: WHITE RABBIT

Years before SMS text messages or email, the suggestion of mobile devices was limited to science-fiction books and movies. Ideas, trends, and fashions did not travel instantly, but migrated slowly around the world. Americans mainly wore blue jeans, and the rest of the world waited for their day to wear them. The new competitive airfares afforded exotic world travel for more and more people. Online travel reservations were a distant dream. The media at the time were limited to network television news, newspapers, radio, and the old reliable word of mouth.

In early 1971, the media often reported frequent demonstrations related to the Vietnam War, the U.S. Army draft system, bra burning, censorship, sex, drugs, graft, pollution, and the environment to name a few important issues. It was a tumultuous period, following the decade of multiple assassinations in the 1960s. The pendulum of life swung wildly. It was a fateful time. The choices made then for many people lasted a lifetime.

While hitchhiking, I heard the news of the San Fernando Valley earthquake, which occurred in the early morning of February 9th in the foothills of the San Gabriel Mountains in southern California. At a magnitude between 6.5 and 6.7, it wasn't small and was one in a series that affected the Los Angeles area in the late 20th century.

Many were drawn to California, the state that spawned hippies. My path led me not to Haight-Ashbury, but to Monterey and its Pier. With a population of slightly less than the current 28,000, Monterey is a quiet, small city. After hearing positive reports from other travelers, this was my choice. Located on California's central coast, Monterey is home to several museums, theaters, arts and crafts venues on Fisherman's Wharf and the well-known Monterey Jazz Festival. The creative flavor of the city was appealing.

Pebble Beach Golf Links was on my list of places to visit. It is commonly regarded as one of the most beautiful golf courses in the world. This suited my quest to visit the best, tallest, loveliest, biggest fill-in-the-blank on my travels. At Pebble Beach, the impressive golf club was as magnificent as the views.

By the third day in Monterey, my new girlfriend Sally and I separated. Our relationship was short-lived, although powerful emotions were triggered. It was a beautiful sunny Californian morning, ideal for a stroll, and I wandered all day in a trance. I regarded it as unwise to leave because a methodical decision is sometimes better than an emotional one. An extra day or two aided clear thinking. My friend Bob now lived in Monterey, and without his address or phone number, I entertained hopes of bumping into him.

By sunset, I had traversed nearly fifteen miles, and it seemed rather pointless. I was close to downtown with its noise and activity when all I craved was somewhere quiet. Tired from my fruitless day, sleep was the answer, and my best option was to head towards my familiar friend, the Monterey Pier.

It was a short jaunt to the waterfront street known as Cannery Row. Originally the location of sardine canning factories, the prior name of the street was Ocean View Avenue until it was renamed Cannery Row in 1958 in honor of John Steinbeck and his famous novel of the same name. The last cannery closed two years after my visit, and the street is now a popular tourist destination, filled with hotels and restaurants, some of which are in the former cannery buildings.

On Cannery Row, I spotted an empty lot surrounded by buildings which was a suitable place to sleep. It was 8:00 p.m., and I was eager for a night of slumber. The location was ideal since the street was quiet, devoid of other people and traffic. Moments away from dreamland, a situation arose illustrating the depth of a friendship is not measured by time.

On the sidewalk, lost in the solitude of my dreamy mind filled with thoughts of rest and sleep, I heard a voice from above. It was not the commanding voice of a higher being, but instead a frantic voice.

"Hey you, down there! Stop!"

Above me was a person leaning out a second-floor window. He was overly agitated.

"Don't go anywhere," he pleaded. "I'll be down in a minute!"

"Okay," I replied.

In a few seconds, he was downstairs and opened the door. He was close to my age and he appeared acutely troubled.

"I need your help," he begged.

"What's the problem?" I asked, puzzled by his urgency.

"I'm having a bad trip."

This explained his erratic behavior; I suspected he was in the process of flipping out. Visibly in a most precarious state of mind and quite desperate, I said I'd join him in the building. My day of confusion now had a definite purpose—to save someone from a bad LSD trip.

In a spartan office with a few desks and chairs, we introduced ourselves; his name was Mark. He immediately launched into his plight. The "infinite numbers" uncontrollably racing through his brain pushed him to the point of near suicide. I was clueless as to what he meant by "infinite numbers" as I sat in front of him, but they had a powerful effect. I attempted to redirect his thoughts to more mundane matters, focused on basic questions with simple answers. This was a helpful approach, and gradually, Mark regained control of his panicked frame of mind. Subsequently, his disposition greatly improved, and we began to have a normal conversation.

Mark was in Monterey for the weekend working on a project at his buddy's office when he flipped out. Mark was a student at Stanford University and Monterey was his weekend getaway for creative solitude.

Our conversation lasted an hour. Then, after a pause, Mark gave me a heartfelt look and stated, "You saved my life." This was the first indication Mark's bad trip ended and his magical mystery tour was a closed chapter. I suspect my presence and companionship were the remedies as opposed to the conversation. Next, he posed the question, "What can I do for you?"

I was relieved Mark recovered intact, and my request was for a place to sleep, suggesting the office was ideal. Unfortunately, it was his friend's office. Mark pondered for a moment before his face lit up.

"Although I'm returning to Stanford tonight at 11:00 p.m., let's go to a party now, and I'll arrange for you to sleep there."

He was pleased with his solution, but the thought of delaying sleep for a few more hours added to my fatigue. This was no ordinary gathering as Mark explained the reasons for the party. He clarified his fascination with numbers in greater detail. He was an 'electronics genius'-the same as everyone at the party since it was exclusively for computer club members. Now the question surfaced: What exactly is a computer and an electronics genius?

I recalled hearing the name UNIVAC computer, and pundits predicted computers to be the next major technological innovation. I occasionally watched science-fiction movies featuring a machine the size of a room with flashing lights which was called a computer. Was this what Mark was referring to? My knowledge of electronics centered around my six-transistor radio, record player, and stereo tuner. From what he portrayed, this party was light years beyond Bowie's social scene, and I was stimulated by the thought of a room full of passionate geniuses. Then there was an unusual twist.

"Since you're not a club member, I'll tell everyone you're an electronics genius like me. What do you think?"

This hippie hitchhiker was not deterred and appreciated the promotion to electronics genius.

"Sure," I confidently answered and accepted the enhanced status in exchange for a comfortable place to sleep.

My initial assumption of a party with dozens of people was grossly inaccurate. Mark and I were the last party attendees. In the living room, there were eight club members. It was not the lively event I pictured, with guests busy socializing and having little opportunity to discuss technical matters.

There was a clear hierarchy among the electronics geniuses, and Mark was at the top. The star of the show, he was unquestionably the most admired and most popular person. I was introduced to one of his friends, and as Mark wandered off, it became more difficult to successfully carry out my role.

Soon, the one friend became four enthusiastic geniuses who gathered around and asked my opinion about the blue box. What on earth was a blue box? What does it have to do with electronics? Now my mind raced on how to respond.

I casually answered, "Sorry guys, I've had enough technical talk tonight with Mark. Let's relax and not discuss the box for now."

They were disappointed by my response, but my strategy shifted the topic of our conversation. After I cracked a few jokes, the tone of the conversation became less businesslike. It was a relief, and I was one step closer to sleep. Many decades later, I learned a blue box was an electronic device that simulated a telephone operator by generating the same tones employed by a human operator's dialing console. In other words, it was a means for free long-distance calling.

It was almost 11:00 p.m. when Mark said everything was arranged for the night. As he left the party, our eyes met, and he flashed a goodbye smile. A special unforgettable smile from someone whose life I saved and one I will never forget.

Mark's group was an early Stanford computer club which became a larger forum for electronic experts to exchange ideas. A later version of the group, called the Homebrew Computer Club, had several future well-known industry leaders, such as Steve Wozniak, Steve Jobs, Paul Allen, and Bill Gates. I believe Mark and his friends had a hand in creating my computer. Our ships passed in the night, and it was the last time I saw Mark.

> *I am looking forward to your visit. It will be joyous to see you again. Once, long ago, we were close. We were one. A moment's perfect match when we met, and you created an instant genius. I do not know the time of your arrival, but we will do everything we missed over the years. It will be like yesterday, and time will roll back like the tide.*

The sun shines over the rolling hills of life beyond my window, and it is brighter for your impending presence. The last of the winter's snowfall melts, and the spring season begins its splendor. The birds are busy proclaiming their joy ... and mine.

I predict your visit will be as magnificent. The places we will go and the conversations we will have. We will walk through the gates of time, not as two older men, but in the prime of our lives—the genius and the hippie. Friends for a moment. Friends for a lifetime.

"Welcome! Come in! It's fantastic to see you, and you haven't changed one bit."

TRACK SEVENTEEN
BOB DYLAN:
MR. TAMBOURINE MAN

L ost in thought, I stared blankly at the Pacific Ocean which I was resolute to cross. Hitchhiking was not an option. My next step was an inexpensive flight to somewhere across the vast expanse of the largest ocean on Earth. The discarded copy of the *San Francisco Chronicle* on the sidewalk bench beside me equaled a Google search at the time. It tempted me with the idea of an inexpensive flight to Honolulu as the next leg of my journey. Hawaii is an additional 2,500 miles from Monterey, leading my island-hopping tour.

First, a short detour back to nature. The call of the wild led to Big Sur, a picturesque spot. A lightly populated region on California's Central Coast, where the Santa Lucia Mountains rise abruptly from the Pacific Ocean, it is located some 28 miles from Monterey.

Pfeiffer Burns State Park piqued my interest. Centered around the Big Sur River, it is often referred to as the 'Mini Yosemite', with an abundance of trees, hiking trails, and campgrounds. It would be a calm setting to wander around and unwind from the stresses of being an electronics genius.

In the afternoon, I exited my ride at the parking lot, which was bustling with activity as campers and hikers arrived and departed. The bathroom facilities and the water fountains were busy. I felt adventurous, off to see the wizard in a sense, as I left the ease and convenience of the facilities and ventured into the interior of the park. My quest was a quiet place to commune with nature. Being enveloped by trees and shrubbery was a welcome escape from the cars and trucks blazing down the highway; the forest beckoned, lovely, dark, and deep.

As I hiked among the greenery with its dappled sunshine and earthy smells, the atmosphere was initially calming as I began my lesson in survival training. I had a canteen full of water, but no food or supplies. It was a sudden power outage kind of moment. This was the place to awaken the skills of a mountain man. The further I ventured, the greater the degree of difficulty in finding food, comfort, and safety. My objective for the day was to test my limits.

After trekking a few miles, I passed other hikers headed to the parking lot and asked which plants were edible along the way. Some fellow day trippers recommended a few so-called 'safe' plants. As my hunger increased, these became an appealing meal. I sampled a few; they were not as appetizing as they initially looked.

My idea to enjoy nature without any supplies now appeared foolish at night. I was unprepared to camp, with only my jacket and trusty small pack with a few bare necessities. I believed in traveling light, and right now that was not a good idea. At this point, I did not have a sleeping bag.

The so-called communal feeling between man and nature was also missing, and I was the lone foolish hiker at night. Keep going, I said to myself. The original purpose of the hike was to unwind, and I was steadfast not to succumb to the call of the park's main entrance with conveniences. Onward, it was a nice evening to tempt fate.

My main concerns were focused on eating and sleeping, and the single path I started on led to many others, adding to the fear of becoming hopelessly lost. To distract myself, I fantasized sensing delicious aromas and sitting around a campfire with a pot of simmering stew. These were the wishful thoughts of a tired and hungry hiker.

I have visions of Robinson Crusoe. Will I ever see another human being? Is anybody out there? The trees seem to close in on me as the temperature drops and my pace quickens. Another stumble. Am I to be food for the forest creatures?

Shapes and shadows. Creaks and moans. What was that? Just my stomach rumbling. Fancy a nice juicy burger? No thanks, I'll take the chicken and fries. Or will it be a wild mushroom and leaf sandwich? Slap! The mosquitoes are feasting on my flesh.

Smoke. I'm hallucinating with hunger. Stumble, mumble. In The Hitchhiker's Manual: Always carry a flashlight when lost in a forest. Slap, stumble, stomach grumble. Smoke. I'm hallucin … No, I'm not! I see light, hear noises. What day is it? Is that you? Smoke and … cooking! Welcome lost stranger; take a seat and have a bite.

My imagination soon became a reality when I stumbled upon two friendly campers who graciously provided food and a spot to sleep next to their campfire. There was a place for a foolish, wandering hiker after all. I was relieved to be in a safe harbor with a hot dinner and lively conversation before bedtime. I rested on Mother Earth as I drifted off to a peaceful sleep next to the warmth of a flickering fire.

The next morning was serene, and as I opened my eyes I witnessed what I missed in the night. The gentle breeze swayed the trees, and the sun's rays flashed through the branches as the morning denizens of the forest began their day with gusto. To my surprise, my camper friends said there was a small earthquake last night. It was a shame to have missed it, sensing the earth's power beneath me for the first time, and gaining a clearer understanding of the extremes lying beneath us.

I was rejuvenated to be on the road and ready to hitchhike to Santa Barbara. The short distance from there to the Los Angeles airport was ideal. I returned to the parking lot and out onto the highway to hitchhike. It was a sunny day, and I was once more the hippie hitchhiker and not the hippie hiker, lost at night.

Soon, a driver named Will stopped, and I was Santa Barbara bound. He was a strong proponent of the burgeoning wine industry in California and elaborated on the wineries in the area which offered free tours, including samples of wine and cheese. California wine did not begin to receive international attention until the mid to late 1970s and thus, in March '71, I was unaware of the state's many wineries. Today, the region's wine annually generates in excess of $30 billion from the sale of close to 300 million cases.

Will recommended a winery to enjoy free samples of wine and local cheeses close to his exit. It was an excellent suggestion for breakfast. After saying goodbye to Will, I soon sipped wine and ate Monterey Jack cheese at a roadside winery. I loved the fact I ate cheese from Monterey, where I was only a few days ago. I doubted it was still made by Mexican Franciscan friars as it had been originally in the 18th century before being sold by Californian businessman David Jack. Today, annual sales are greater than $100 million.

When I left the winery, it wasn't long before I had a ride to Santa Barbara. The driver, Carl, recently returned from his U.S. Marine tour of Vietnam, which included being involved in the Battle of Khe Sanh. This was the lengthiest, deadliest, and most controversial battle of the entire Vietnam War, as the U.S. Marines and their allies fought the North Vietnamese Army and lost.

It began in late January '68 and in *Time* magazine's April 12th edition, their *Victory at Khe Sanh* article quoted General William Westmoreland,

Commander of U.S. forces in Vietnam, who stated: "We took 220 killed at Khe Sanh and roughly 800 wounded and evacuated. The enemy by my count suffered at least 15,000 dead in the area." Later, the unofficial totals came close to 1,000 U.S. forces KIA.

It was obvious the impact of the battle was a dilemma for Carl after his base was overrun by the North Vietnamese Army. He spoke of his sadness to witness the high price many young Americans paid in Vietnam, and he had the thousand-mile look soldiers suffer after horrific battles. I saw glimpses of the old Carl when he reminisced about his girlfriend and his job in the days prior to enlisting in the U.S. Marines. Carl survived the Battle of Khe Sanh, but his new battle was to survive life's aftershocks; what is now called PTSD.

Santa Barbara, nestled between the Santa Ynez Mountains and the Pacific Ocean, was my home for the next week. It is a year-round tourist destination appealing to both mountain and beach lovers. The city is also known as the 'American Riviera" with its Mediterranean climate and Spanish architecture.

My days were spent frequenting wineries and working odd jobs to save $80.00. I visited a few travel agencies, and a one-way student ticket to Honolulu from Los Angeles cost $75.00. This price was one-third the cost of a standard ticket. I left Santa Barbara on a Sunday, after a tall stack of pancakes for breakfast.

The hitchhike to Los Angeles was only 95 miles. The driver on my last ride before the airport remarked, "You are lucky, this is the first smog-free day in a long time." I interpreted that to be a good thing. In the airport by 11:00 a.m., I had four hours before my flight was scheduled to depart. Bored and anxious, I meandered around the terminal and found a stack of Sunday *Los Angeles Times* newspapers near a dumpster. I grabbed ten and sold all of them by the escalator. Plenty to buy lunch and a few beers.

Oh, the little joys of flying. There was a contest on the flight for passengers to correctly guess the duration of the flight to Honolulu, and I won second prize with my guess of 5 hours, 20 minutes, and 23 seconds. I was now the proud owner of four Mai Tai cups. The first prize winner won $25.00; his guess was ten seconds closer than mine. When I exited the airport doors, I had a couple of dollars in my pocket and my set of Mai Tai cups. Aloha Hawaii.

The plane landed at 8:00 p.m., and all was quiet outside the airport. There were few cars on the road to Honolulu, and I was alone on the bus stop bench. A taxicab exceeded my tight budget, and it was unlikely I could trade my Mai Tai cups for a ride. A taxicab stopped, and the driver offered a ride to Honolulu. I explained my dire straits.

"If you're waiting for the bus, the next one isn't until tomorrow morning. Climb aboard, I'll give you a free ride!" the friendly driver said. As soon as I closed the door, he added, "If you reach into the glove box, there's some pot. Let's have a smoke to welcome you to Honolulu!" I breezed into Waikiki, stoned and happy!

TRACK EIGHTEEN
THE DOORS: LIGHT MY FIRE

Waikiki is the beachfront neighborhood of Honolulu on the south side of Oahu Island. The singer and entertainer Don Ho was a fixture at the Waikiki Beachcomber on Kalakaua Avenue, Waikiki's main street named after King Kalakaua. This was where I left the easygoing taxi driver with a handshake and a wave goodbye. The adjustment to my new surroundings, combined with jet lag, would be tackled in the morning. An empty hammock behind a house a few blocks from the beach was where I found a place to sleep.

It was almost as quiet the next morning as it had been the previous night. The sounds of the surf played to a deserted beach, and the parade of tourists amounted to me and a few dozen people. I was welcomed by the warm trade winds and pleasant temperatures. My first mission was breakfast and then finding a more permanent place called home. This entailed asking what became standard questions in my travels.

"Where do hippies gather? Where is the best place to work? Where is the safest and least expensive place to live?"

An early morning hippie I encountered recommended a local hangout which was a nearby convenience store and mentioned temporary work was available at Manpower, a work placement company. The reason for limited options to sleep for free was due to the popularity of Honolulu.

I was advised to not camp on the beach. Apparently, people sleeping on the beach were frequently rousted from their slumbers by the local constabulary.

I visited the YMCA for a shower and shave before tackling the chore of establishing a home base. First on the list was collecting soda bottles for the one cent return deposit. I was hungry; my last meal was on the flight. I wasn't the only person searching, judging by the dearth of soda bottles. The rear of the hippie-central convenience store was a gold mine of empty bottles. After collecting a few bottles, I exchanged them for cash at the front of the store.

Although what I did was less than honest, hunger was the main catalyst for my action, and this ill-gotten money paid for breakfast. This escapade created a new tenet to live by: I will never allow hunger to drive irrational behavior which carries with it the possibility of arrest. No matter what the circumstances, I promised to eat a minimum of two meals per day honestly. All my meals were obtained without being dishonest from that day forward.

My remaining goals for the day were a job and a home. The rest was easy once those two objectives were accomplished. I acquired an application from the clerk at Manpower, less than two miles from Waikiki. He recommended to be there the following morning at 7:00 a.m. when potential workers would be given a number in the order of arrival for the jobs' roll call.

With the early morning roll call, the best option was camping in this neighborhood. Manpower was in an isolated warehouse district. I inquired about free lodging with several locals, and one gentleman was the owner of a surfboard shop. He granted permission to camp in the backyard of his shop, which was three-blocks from Manpower. So far, so good.

During my first week in Honolulu, while I camped behind the surfboard shop, it was a mile to shower at the YMCA. On the third morning, the

YMCA front desk clerk informed me the facilities were for members only.

"Well, if that is your policy, I will shower at the Hilton hotel," I replied with more bravado than sense.

Determined to be true to my word, I strolled into the Hilton lobby elevator and went to the 6th floor. Six happened to be the first number to catch my eye on the bank of numbers in the elevator. Down the hallway, I spotted an open door where the maid was cleaning the room. I slipped silently into the room and strode into the bathroom unnoticed by the maid, who was busy vacuuming around a king-sized bed. I closed the bathroom door, showered, and hung the bath towel on the rack. I peered out the bathroom door as the maid vacuumed the room. With her back facing me, I exited the room, cleaner and fresher.

With my first job via Manpower, my duties at a meat processing facility for two days were combining fat and hunks of beef into a grinder to produce tons of ground beef for hamburgers. My third day was spent moving heavy boxes at Hickam Air Force Base. By the fourth day, I was sent across the street from Manpower to a small mom and pop company named Crown & Co., a manufacturer known for their quality louvered doors and shutters.

Their morning tasks included sweeping and cleaning the warehouse, and moving what needed to be moved—paint, boxes, shutters, doors, etc.—alongside the only other worker, a young man named Phil. At 12:30 p.m., Phil and I left for our lunch break at a local diner. During our casual conversation, the topic was my around the world trip. He was curious to hear more, and I shared with him my story of how I hitchhiked across the U.S. and now I was in the next phase of my trip.

"I think I can help you," he said, and I was intrigued. "My father owns Crown & Co. and we are hiring a spray painter."

This was an opportune gesture if I was a spray painter; however, Phil said it was on the job training, and my lack of experience was inconsequential. The next day I became an apprentice spray painter of louvered doors and shutters. Now I had a job, a home was my next mission, in order to replace my camp site behind the surf shop.

I searched the newspaper classifieds every day for an affordable place to live and, after two more nights in the surf shop yard, I noticed an ad for room and board at a boarding house close to the University of Hawaii on Hoonanea St. It sounded perfect.

I was given a tour of the available room, the boarding house, and other amenities. All the other lodgers were Japanese. A possible novel and fun experience was in store. I submitted the application and paid $90.00 for the first month's rent, which included breakfast and dinner daily. A home *and* two meals a day resolved.

The view from my bedroom window was of Diamond Head and a glimpse of the Pacific Ocean. The news every few weeks reported two people on the scenic overlook at Diamond Head and one mysteriously fell off the cliff. The other person walked down the hill never to be found. My amateur guess was this was a quickie divorce Hawaiian style. The other popular news story was lone hikers disappearing off the trails after becoming trapped in a jungle of vines and underbrush, better described as a human mouse trap.

Among all the boarders, there were a few large sumo-sized men, and I was the skinniest. For some reason, the cook believed it was her duty to increase my food portions to the extent I consumed double and triple the amount of food as my fellow comrades. After weeks of these extra servings, my weight remained the same, much to the astonishment of everyone at the dinner table.

The work at Crown & Co. was particularly memorable, especially two notable jobs. The first was an all-expenses paid project to assist Monty, the chief installer/spray painter, at the Volcano House hotel in the Hawaii Volcanoes National Park on the big island. The 505-square mile national park is home to two active and notable volcanoes, Kilauea and

Mauna Loa. Kilauea is one of the world's most active volcanoes, and Mauna Loa is the most massive shield volcano in the world.

The Volcano House hotel was our home for the next three days while we installed louvered shutters. I said this was "cool", but Monty suggested that was not an accurate description of volcanoes! This was the beginning of my love for and fascination with volcanoes, visiting dozens in my future travels. Although daunting in size and power, there is also something magical about them. There is no other marvel to better demonstrate the strength of Mother Nature, and Monty was right when I considered the 200 megatons explosive force which creates lava flows reaching 2,000°F or higher.

The setting for the hotel, situated on the rim of Kilauea, was unique, and it did not occur to me a hotel could be safely built on the rim of a volcano. As Monty and I walked out onto the less active part of the crater, sulfur spewed as we were encircled by gigantic rocks the size of cars. The air had an unpleasant rotten egg odor and, as if in a lunar landscape, we were surrounded by the high walls of the crater. With aspirations of adventure, I chuckled at the possibility of one small step for me and one giant leap for hippie-kind.

I love rock music, but I don't always like rocks since crazy people can throw them at you. Rocks are hard, and they hurt. Wrong! Yes, they hurt but aren't always hard! "But how?" I hear you say, and I answer, "Volcanoes, because they erupt molten rock!

What person of any age can't be impressed with something seemingly solid as a rock coming out of the ground molten! Lava, that glowing orange river, starts as molten rock formed deep inside our planet.

The souvenirs for a poor backpacker are intangible treasures: chance meetings, memories, learned lessons, friendships, and love. I leave Hawaii with a lasting respect and fascination for volcanoes, which my three days on the rim of the Kilauea volcano cemented. I am awestruck by the power and beauty manifested by its illustrious size and shape.

As I write about these slumbering giants now, someone first drew a picture of one more than 8,000 years ago. They fascinated then and they fascinate now. Maybe they fascinate aliens too because they're not only on our planet.

Others say a volcano is merely a pimple on the face of the planet. I, on the other hand, appreciate its exquisiteness. To visit a volcano is to peek below the surface of the world. As the heat rises, I gaze into the crater and see its majestic splendor. It is all-encompassing, uplifting my senses to euphoria. Thank you, Hawaii, for the best souvenir ever.

Most of our installation work was in Kahala, where some of the finest homes and condominiums in Honolulu are located, and my second memorable job was at the home of Jack Lord, the star of *Hawaii Five-0*. This popular television police drama aired from 1968 to 1980, and Jack Lord's portrayal of Detective Captain Steve McGarrett was immortalized by the phrase, "Book 'em, Danno" as he instructed his subordinate to arrest the criminal.

When installing louvered shutters in Mr. Lord's condominium, I hoped to meet him, but only the maid was home. However, during the period I lived in Hawaii, I often saw the crew filming the show in different Honolulu neighborhoods, generally Waikiki and Kahala, and I enjoyed watching the series and recognizing familiar places. At the airing of its last episode, the show was the longest-running police series in the history of American television.

I adjusted quickly to the routine of Crown & Co. and my home creature comforts. I loved living in the 50th state; the weather, ocean, and culture were all ideal. My tranquil time in Hawaii was a contrast to key events on the mainland during the period. A bomb exploded in a men's room

THE DOORS: LIGHT MY FIRE

at the U.S. Capitol and thousands of protesters were arrested at the May Day Protests in Washington, D.C., the largest mass arrest in U.S. history. U.S. Army Lieutenant William Calley was found guilty of 22 murders in the My Lai massacre, and Charles Manson was sentenced to death. Manson's sentence was commuted to life imprisonment after California invalidated the state's death penalty statute in 1972.

On my days off, considerable time was spent in the local library where I studied many travel books and maps to select the best itinerary. At a desk adjacent to the gigantic floor world globe that dominated the library's reading room, it was exhilarating to contemplate the possibilities for this leg of my adventure.

There were travel guides for upscale tourists, yet none existed to speak of for backpackers in my era. Today, there are many online resources for the solo traveler. My primary concern was what to expect at the next destination. What are the pitfalls? What is the culture? Where do backpackers hang out? Are there job prospects?

The 'tourist trail' refers to informal routes from continent to continent used by many backpackers. All this information was word of mouth, similar to tour guide tips, and consisted of taking the ferry instead of flying, visiting this worthwhile place, etc. On the tourist trail, discussions with other travelers who had first-hand knowledge about various destinations were invaluable. The information garnered oftentimes was a lifesaver, especially quirks and differences in laws, jobs, and culture.

There are many tourist destinations today (for example, Koh Samui, Thailand, and Goa, India) that became popular thanks to hippies. This first wave of tourists and backpackers couldn't afford popular five-star destinations, and they gravitated toward budget-friendly exotic locales despite limited services and accommodations. These were the pioneers who initiated the chain of events for these then small resorts to grow and prosper.

In Honolulu, I met some fellow travelers, and Jody spoke of New Zealand. He said jobs were plentiful there and described the country and some of his experiences. Jody and I were at opposite ends of our travels, with me beginning my journey as he was ending his. It was fitting to trade my folding wallet for Jody's handmade kangaroo passport holder, which I still use five decades later. Let's hope his wallet has lasted as long.

To quench my wanderlust, I inquired at travel agencies as to the best fare from Honolulu to Auckland. There was an inexpensive flight from Honolulu to Pago Pago in American Samoa, Suva in Fiji, and Auckland, New Zealand. My other travel options were South Korea, then onward to Russia on the Trans-Siberian railroad toward Europe, or Tokyo. Japan was a possibility due to the abundance of English teaching jobs. The more westerly routes were less attractive, mainly due to visa requirements and expensive fares.

Leaving Hawaii signaled the conclusion of a perfect chapter in my travels. It meant the end of regular meals with my friends, abandoning my newfound water bed, the view of Diamond Head and the tranquility I had obtained in Hawaii. I felt a sense of loss and second guessed my move as I embarked towards my next destination. But I was hooked on travel, and adventure overruled logic.

In a few days, I resigned from my job, bought my plane ticket, and said goodbye to my friends. I had $50.00 to cover expenses until Auckland, New Zealand. Before my departure from the boarding house, I gave the cook my Mai-Tai cups as a parting gift.

TRACK NINETEEN
LED ZEPPELIN: RAMBLE ON

On June 29th, 1971, I advanced hesitantly toward the ticket counter at the Honolulu airport. With the final surge of mixed emotions, I was happy to go and sad to leave. As I write these words five decades later, the memories of my friends, experiences, happiness, and sadness have the same intensity. My daily life in Hawaii was appealing; however, the goal of traveling around the world ruled the day.

I slowly handed my ticket to the agent with trepidation, and she systematically removed the stub with finality. I received the boarding pass and gate number, now committed to boarding the airplane. Like a racehorse jockey entering the starting gate, anxiously waiting for the bell to ring, I sat in the departure lounge with my mind in a tizzy and then turned to my right …

Beside me was the most attractive woman, and instantly, as sparks flew, our conversation became electric. She exuded vibrancy, and I was captivated by her presence, fighting all my natural instincts to follow this woman onto her flight to the mainland, which was departing from the adjacent gate. Then my flight to Pago Pago was announced.

With a final look of what might have been, we parted. While my temptation was stretched to capacity, I coaxed my unwilling legs toward the roar of the beckoning jet engines. The die was cast, my decision was made, and there was no room for deviation. The siren called, and it was hard to resist. As with meeting friends in faraway places, I believed such an incident was rare, and yet this was the first of several similar encounters minutes before boarding a flight.

The first segment of my journey to New Zealand brought me to Pago Pago, the capital of American Samoa. With my inexpensive airfare, I flew 2,608 miles further south from Hawaii and 7,000 miles from Bowie. A short distance southeast of Western Samoa (a New Zealand territory in 1971), American Samoa is an unincorporated territory of the U.S. This means it is controlled by the U.S. Government but is not part of the U.S., and today, is one of the thirteen U.S. territories, which include Guam and Puerto Rico.

The plane landed in Pago Pago at 8:00 p.m. and the tourist information kiosk in the tiny airport was closed. It is preferable to arrive in the day since there is an intricate art to locating a safe place to sleep and finding cheap eats. The level of difficulty increases dramatically at night.

Outside the airport, I hopped on the local bus to Pago Pago, nine miles away. I was the lone passenger who exited the bus in the heart of town. It was a small plaza, consisting of a post office, convenience store, administrative building, and a single hitching rail for horses. In an instant, I was transported to a Western movie set instead of being on an island in the South Pacific. The few buildings were one and two stories high, and the square was dark and deserted. This was unusual for an early evening.

I pondered the latest predicament on where to hang my hat. In my trance, the answer popped out in the shape of a lone man who emerged from the other end of the plaza.

"Hello there, can you recommend a place to sleep?" I asked.

He suggested the InterContinental Hotel, a secluded luxury resort one block away. American budget-oriented backpackers were rare. In this period, most Americans were perceived as affluent compared to other nationalities. I was a camper, a key detail I initially neglected to mention. With only the two of us in the square, the man leaned forward and said the hotel permitted their employees to sleep on the poolside sunbeds at night.

The pool at the hotel was easy to locate, and after a long flight, sleep was my main objective. I selected my sunbed for the night and slept soundly except for a few friendly wake-up reminders from the resort staff in the middle of the night.

"Excuse me, sir," said the voice, interrupting my dream.

I was half-asleep as the hotel employee suggested, "Perhaps you should return to your room."

"Okay, thank you," I mumbled in response.

At sunrise, I viewed my surroundings for the first time. There were a number of private bungalows and a spacious cabana with dining tables, where waiters busily prepared a breakfast buffet. Beyond the hotel was the ocean and tree-lined mountains. In 1971, the cost per night was $50.00, equivalent to $300.00 per night today. The hotel was five-star living, nestled between Pago Pago Bay and Rainmaker Mountain.

I dreamily wandered to the open-air market to buy tasty fruit for breakfast. After the market, I didn't have a care in the world. I sauntered from palm tree to palm tree and then sat under a majestic one for hours, basking in the shade to the sweet-sounding ocean surf. As the incoming tide gently rolled in, laughing children splashed in the shimmering blue water. It was a lazy, mellow day. Later in the evening at the hotel, I watched the evening entertainment show featuring local Polynesian dancers. The lively performance was incomparable. I was transfixed by the energetic stamina of the dancers, their radiant costumes, and the nonstop pulsing tempo of the music.

The hotel employees understood I was merely a happy hippie camper, and my restful sleep during the second night was undisturbed. I appreciated traveling with one small backpack. To the untrained eye, it appeared my bag held the contents of daily pool gear.

Poolside under the sun, moon, and stars was the perfect home. One afternoon, an annoyed hotel guest questioned how I landed the best poolside location every day. I casually shrugged and replied, "I'm an early riser."

The favorable climate, with daytime temperatures around 80°F and 70°F at night, coupled with ocean breezes created a comfortable poolside locale and neighborhood. It was an ideal place to relax and unwind and compared to camping in Ocho Rios, Jamaica, my new accommodation was a significant improvement. Staying in an established five-star resort for free was a far better option than a five-star resort yet to be built.

Some mornings, I ate a nice breakfast at the poolside cabana. For $1.40, I treated myself to two eggs served with bacon or sausage. Other mornings I ordered hotcakes for 75 cents and fresh papaya for an additional 35 cents. The native fare was delicious, with plenty of local seafood, especially tuna. A local restaurateur said Pago Pago was home to Chicken of the Sea and StarKist, two of the largest tuna processors.

Thirty minutes later, on an unexplored street, I recognized the colorful sign depicting Charlie the Tuna, StarKist's cartoon mascot. If you are unfamiliar with the advertisement, Charlie was repeatedly rejected by StarKist because he claimed to have good taste. However, StarKist did not want tuna with good taste, they wanted tuna that tasted good.

My favorite dinner was traditional oka, fresh fish marinated in coconut milk, served with tomatoes and cucumbers. Fresh fruits were also readily available, including coconuts and passionfruit. Sampling local delicacies is a guaranteed formula for good eats at bargain prices, a practice I still adhere to today. When I skipped breakfast in the hotel, I purchased large meals at the local market for $1.00 or less.

I walked, hitchhiked, or rode the bus as I toured the island during the day. The hot sun, surf, and mile after mile of empty beaches punctuated the scenery. A fleeting thought was to legally work in a U.S. territory. I left Hawaii with $50.00 and allocated $25.00 to cover my stay in American Samoa and an equal amount for my next stop in Fiji. The beach bum life on these two islands was my assignment before working in New Zealand. I was employed for three months in Hawaii, and a vacation was well-deserved. I'd address my lack of funds in New Zealand. For now, freedom, rest, and relaxation were on the agenda.

With its friendly atmosphere, pristine beaches, quiet small towns, and villages, I found American Samoa to be a hidden gem. It boasts one of the world's largest natural harbors and today, cruise ships transport 31,000 visitors yet only 3,000 tourists arrive independently every year. I do not know how many tourists visited in 1971, but the island's population density was 100 people per square kilometer, with a population of 27,292. For comparison, today there are nearly 54,000 *daily* visitors to Walt Disney World Magic Kingdom in Florida.

The tranquility of American Samoa was interrupted only once during my time at the hotel—on Rainmaker Mountain, an unexploded ordnance from World War II was detonated without warning. This disruption lasted only a minute, causing a minor blip in everyone's holiday before they recommenced their more important activities of swimming, suntanning, and drinking.

The ocean, mountains, flora, fauna, and other elements of nature combined to produce an idyllic place to unwind. The decision to leave Hawaii now made sense. I searched for serenity, and American Samoa provided an ideal place. It was a tropical paradise which delivered rest and relaxation, with the bonus of 'camping' in a luxury resort.

Two or three planes per day departed or landed on the island, and airport traffic remains low today. My flight to Fiji left once a week, and I considered extending my stay, but on July 3rd, I said goodbye to

American Samoa. At the airport two hours before my scheduled flight, I was the first passenger in the terminal.

With little to do in the small airport, I headed towards the ocean along the length of the only runway. At the end was a grassy area a few feet from the edge of a rocky fifty-foot cliff. I was drawn by the noise of the ocean and became entranced by the mesmeric force of the incoming waves, whose spray covered me in a fine mist like a refreshing shower.

With relentless, pounding energy, and a roar akin to the jet engines that would soon soar down the runway, the waves crashed into v-shaped vents blasting into the lower face. They slammed the cliff wall with such ferocity, ostensibly providing a glimpse into eternity. I was one step from the abyss. Six gigantic and powerful geysers shot thirty feet above the ground behind me, before collapsing and receding dramatically with equal force.

This awesome phenomenon occurred every thirty seconds. I was entranced by the power of the ocean coupled with the magnificence of the geysers' display as I observed it from the edge of the cliff. My senses were magnified until I became giddy with laughter. It was similar to a young child riding a rollercoaster, feeling excited and terrified at the same time. The commanding force of the ocean, like volcanoes, demonstrated the power of nature compared to man.

I said goodbye to Pago Pago as I headed across the International Date Line, traveling 800 miles from the equator and south to Suva, Fiji. This was another short stopover to sightsee and contemplate the upcoming dilemma of being broke. I had $25.00 in my pocket and remembered the time when $10.00 lasted two weeks in Europe.

This beautiful island in the Pacific Ocean was my next stop. I left the peace and quiet of American Samoa to experience the wider ethnic diversity, busier traffic, and greater tourist activity of the Fijian capital, and the island's largest metropolitan city. The hustle and bustle of commerce rushing towards the apex of the future, that was Suva.

Fiji is an archipelago consisting of 330 islands, and in 1970, the population was 520,000. Predominantly native Fijians of Melanesian and Polynesian descent, there was also a large Indian population due to the influx of laborers brought to the islands by the British in the 19th century. When I visited in 1971, the island was newly self-governing after Britain had granted independence to it one year earlier.

Fiji is known for its jagged landscapes, palm tree beaches, coral reefs, and vibrant lagoons. At this point in my travels, this was another lovely Pacific island. The sun, beaches, ocean, and exotic feel were pleasingly familiar. I was fascinated to read Captain Bligh sailed for his life through these islands shortly after the mutiny on the Bounty, barely escaping capture by pursuing cannibals.

After landing in Suva, I maintained my knack of locating an inexpensive place to eat and sleep. For the equivalent of 50 U.S. cents, I had a delectable Indian fish stew for dinner and then slept in a church the first night. The next morning, I visited the open-air market where I sampled fresh watermelon and passionfruit. I also tried Fijian longan or dawa, which is like lychee, with a sweet and refreshing taste. Once more, I was not disappointed by sampling fresh, local fare.

> *As I amble along towards the market, something reflects the morning sun a few paces ahead of me. A lone silver dime straddles two sidewalk squares, creating a bridge between two identical halves. I am reminded of the two sides of our brain and their different functions, working perfectly in tandem in wondrous fashion.*

> *The scientists of the world are diligently studying the mechanical thoughts of the brain, and the answer lies at our feet. I take one big step over defeat and the dime is mine. Find a penny, pick it up, and all day long you'll have good luck. Since this is a dime, my good fortune will be tenfold. My eyes cast downward at my feet, moving step by step.*

It is curious to see a dime in such a position, vulnerable to
the many pedestrians on this delightful day, one to be filled
with luck for me. Seven years ago, the government stopped
minting silver coins, and that dime of old now in my pocket
is priceless. The only explanation for a silver dime on the
sidewalk is that it fell from heaven.

Although Suva has a few parks and gardens, I yearned for a quieter atmosphere similar to Pago Pago. I rode a bus out of town in search of greener pastures to a picturesque place, approximately forty miles west of Suva on the southern coast, called Pacific Harbour (the spelling follows British English).

This town was in the early stages of development, with new residences catering to both expats and locals. Today, it is known as the adventure capital of Fiji, a destination for adrenaline-pumping tourists who choose to swim with sharks or venture off-road on a four-wheel drive excursion.

The area was unquestionably an explorer's delight, full of farmlands, gorges, canyons, rapids, and waterfalls. There was also a tropical rainforest nearby, and it was breathtaking to see herons and various other exotic birds alongside the backdrop of the clear blue sky and the sparkling blue-green ocean. It was a calm oasis of nature, perfect for meditation.

It was several days of solitude, sleeping out in the open and rarely encountering other travelers. I was an island on an island. While I typically met other tourists and shared experiences, those few days provided much appreciated time for myself. The tranquil surroundings recharged my mental and physical batteries for the next leg.

Today, Fiji is an upscale tropical vacation destination, full of world-class resorts, private beaches, and exclusive spas. Affluent natives and expats live in multi-million-dollar villas along the coast of the island, which is regarded as the 'soft coral capital of the world'. It attracts divers and snorkelers from around the world, and it was auspicious to visit this exotic locale for days in virtual solitude.

The bus ride from Pacific Harbour to Suva airport left $2.00 in my pocket. The bus fare and an airport tax were unexpected expenses. The trepidation upon leaving Fiji was a double-edged sword. I was well-rested, but I was concerned about immigration in New Zealand without an onward plane ticket or sufficient funds to enter the country. These are the two rules a backpacker knows never to violate, since deportation home is the consequence.

My success in gaining free entry into music festivals might now be helpful to enter a foreign country. I remembered my U.S. Postal Service uniform and the mindset of Frank Zappa's personal mailman for overcoming the potential obstacle of a zealous Immigration Officer in New Zealand.

Before boarding my flight, I thought how the South Pacific islands were heaven. I was a tiny speck in a huge ocean looking out into the universe. On all the islands I visited, the unexpected good fortune arose like a mighty geyser, rocketing towards the sky.

TRACK TWENTY
THE WHO: GOING MOBILE

I boarded the Air New Zealand flight from Fiji to Auckland with a deep sense of dread. It was not the onset to the fear of flying; I faced the possibility of deportation to Honolulu. I prayed for good fortune, and the flight was smooth and trouble-free. Perhaps this was an omen.

The passport control desks were orderly, and a short line sidestepped worries and visions of handcuffs. I handed my passport to the immigration officer, a somewhat surly gentleman. With a furrowed brow, he scanned my details, compared my features to the photo, and then his expression changed.

"Welcome to New Zealand," he said, handing me my passport, duly appended with a tourist visa stamp. I acknowledged his greeting and stepped forward, breathing a huge sigh of relief. This was a major hurdle cleared, dodging a premature end to my latest leg of travel around the world. I ventured outside the airport, and my newfound sense of well-being came face to face with reality.

How ill-prepared I was for arriving in Auckland in the winter without a coat! I left the 90-degree temperature in Fiji, traveled 1,336 miles south, and lost 60 degrees. My love for occasionally traveling light yelled its downsides from the rooftops. I changed my meager funds to New Zealand dollars and rode the bus downtown to buy a secondhand coat.

Upon arrival on Queen Street in the mid-afternoon, my quest began for warmth. With false hope and optimism, I bolted into a department store and had funds to purchase only the buttons on an enticing sheepskin jacket. I inquired the whereabouts of a secondhand clothing store and was directed to the Ponsonby neighborhood, a mile away.

As I left the store, the radio announced the weather forecast for the coldest night of the year, with temperatures in the low 30s Fahrenheit (below 0 Celsius) due in the evening. This was not encouraging news. It was a race to find a coat or a cold, miserable night was in store for me.

Several store clerks mentioned Ponsonby as a location with many secondhand stores. After my fruitless shopping downtown, I hoofed it to Ponsonby, feeling the air turning colder with every step. It was now 5:00 p.m. with the sun setting. My adrenaline increased, which had a slightly warming effect, or maybe it was the uphill walk. My high hopes of secondhand clothing stores were soon dashed. Nevertheless, I visited several stores for a coat, and the puzzled clerks replied they couldn't help. Ponsonby was home to many secondhand *furniture* stores, not clothing stores.

In 1971, Ponsonby was an inner-city suburb of Auckland, regarded as a less than desirable neighborhood. It was a low rent area, full of rundown buildings and secondhand stores. This contrasts with the present day where, post-gentrification, Ponsonby has become an upper-middle-class residential area, well-known for its dining and shopping venues, art galleries, and nightclubs.

In desperation, I darted into another secondhand furniture store with the possibility of a recommendation of a clothing store nearby.

"Sorry, I can't help you," advised a middle-aged man. "You won't find a secondhand clothing store in this area."

By now, the anguish on my face was evident. He introduced himself as Carmichael, the owner. "Make yourself at home. A couple of friends will be here for a few beers. Why don't you join us?" he asked.

His intuition was accurate. As he hung the closed sign, Carmichael said I was not the first backpacker to wander into his store. After drinking beers and discussing the virtues of rugby versus American football, his friends left, and Carmichael offered the spare room above his store.

He supplied a large pile of furniture dust sheets and an old mattress before he went home. I was certain (at least hoping) any creatures residing among the ancient bed springs would be as friendly as Carmichael. Thank goodness for my in-flight meals to bypass hunger until breakfast. One travel tip imparted from a stewardess: Requests for second meals are generally granted, when available.

The following morning, my most generous landlord returned with a brown paper bag.

"I brought you some tucker," he said.

Inside the bag was a sandwich with thickly-cut fresh bread and equally chunky slices of locally produced cheese. I once more marveled at the kindness shown to lost wandering wayfarers.

Carmichael was inquisitive about my travels, and while devouring the delicious breakfast, I retold my journey which brought me to his door and my present intention to live in New Zealand. I mentioned my profession was a spray painter, whereupon he called his friend at a paint store. It was unfortunate that the qualifications required at least two years of experience. In his effort to help, Carmichael thrust the previous day's newspaper into my hands, opened to the classified ads.

A car washer position at Tasman Rent-a-Car sounded promising. I called the company and scheduled a job interview for the next morning. Now, pursuit switched from employment to a coat. As I explored Ponsonby Road in the morning, I found secondhand clothing stores didn't exist. I surmised people sold or donated furniture but kept a tight fist on their clothing. It was a pleasurable sightseeing trip to downtown Queen Street on a quest for a coat but as expected, nothing was available in my price range. Nevertheless, I was one step closer to a job and a home.

In the mid-afternoon at Carmichael's, he was chatting with five Australian friends, introduced as Lionel, Archie, Simon, Gabriel, and Willy. They all lived nearby and were Aussie draft dodgers shunning the Vietnam War. A total of 60,000 Australian soldiers served in Vietnam until 1972, and it was Australia's longest war until the more recent conflict in Afghanistan. During the period, New Zealand became a haven for Aussies avoiding military service in an unpopular war.

It was the beginning of our friendship. They were inquisitive to my connection to Carmichael, and I repeated the desperate coat story. Lionel grinned and said, "Yank, I have an old coat for you." Kiwis (New Zealanders), Aussies, and Brits refer to Americans as Yanks, not just those from the northeastern region of the U.S.

It was another night above Carmichael's shop, and the next morning, before my interview, I read a newspaper article describing the grand opening of Disney World in Orlando, Florida. Two years ago, when I lived in Orlando, the entertainment complex was under construction. I generally heard news months after an event due to the expense of international newspapers ($1.00) and magazines ($2.00) and lack of a television.

A glance at the old railway station clock ticking loudly on the wall signaled I had ten minutes, so I resumed studying the classified ads for an apartment to rent. There was an ad for a boarding house for $30.00 a month which prompted an immediate call to the phone number listed. I was astonished it was in the same neighborhood. The rental was on Clarence Street, two blocks around the corner from Carmichael's, and an appointment was arranged for later in the afternoon. The attractions of a boarding house are two home cooked meals a day, and a quiet, comfortable place to live—a perfect combination.

At Tasman Rent-a-Car, I was introduced to Alfred, the hiring manager. The interview lasted ten minutes before I was hired, and work began the next morning at 8:00 a.m. My duties were washing, detailing, and driving rental cars to the airport. My salary was $30.00 a week, my lowest salary to date; however, it covered my expenses. Compared with my Aussie friends who earned $20.00 a week, I lucked into a plum job.

The boarding house became my new home. The location was convenient, a one-mile walk to work. A coat, a job, and a new home were mine in a few days. I gave myself a high five.

After my second week of work, I opened a bank account at the ANZ Bank and deposited the majority my salary. Ka-ching! This new bank account heralded the metamorphosis from backpacker to bourgeoisie. To repay the kindness shown by Carmichael and the five Aussies, I treated all of us to fish and chips. This caused an impromptu chorus of the "The Yank's a Jolly Good Fellow!"

On my way home with Lionel, I was stunned to hear that Carmichael was recently released from prison for murder. He was involved in a bar fight where he fatally stabbed a patron. He served ten years in prison and subsequently quit drinking. It was disturbing news, but this revelation did not lessen my gratitude for his assistance. Carmichael was a Maori, a member of the indigenous tribe of Eastern Polynesians in New Zealand and among the fascinating stories he regaled was of the moa. This flightless bird, endemic to New Zealand, was now extinct due to excessive hunting and consumption by Maoris.

It was an easy adjustment to life in Auckland. This lovely pedestrian-friendly port city offered plenty of pubs, fish and chip shops, scenic parks, and much more. Cars in Auckland were predominantly British imports, and Casey, with whom I worked at Tasman, was the proud original owner of a forty-year-old Austin 7. Produced from 1922 until 1939, it became one of the most well-known automobiles manufactured in the UK, similar in popularity to the Model T Ford in the US. Some in the U.S. associate this manufacturer with English cabs.

Casey noted there were many Austin 7s owned for thirty to forty years, a testament to the reliability of the vehicle. In addition, these vehicles were easy to repair, and in 1937, the car company specifically targeted female drivers. With what would now be regarded as sexist advertising, the company promoted it as "The Car for The Feminine Touch" since mechanical knowledge was not necessary for some repairs. On my daily walks to work, I admired many 40-year-old Austins on the road.

The alcoholic beverage of choice was beer based on its cost of 10 cents a pint. In the days before the TV sitcom *Cheers*, our lives were much the same. Some pubs were for men only, but not our 'local' pub. Our after-work ritual was to head directly to the nearby pub to join a few friends for drinks before going home.

We were an eclectic bunch of characters, and sometimes, we partied all night, and a pub crawl ensued around the area. On those nights, a convenient stop after leaving the pub was an outdoor urinal along the sidewalk. The enclosed urinal had a shoulder-high window to see pedestrians and cars, a design which still baffles me to this day.

I happily settled into my new routine of work, socializing and exploring in my free time, and all was normal in Auckland until the brewery strike. Beer sales halted, and a 10-cent pint of beer skyrocketed to $1.00 on the black market. It was Prohibition style beer-buying in dark alleys. I saved extra money by curtailing my drinking habits during this period of high prices and minimal supply, and it was a tense time for citizens until the strike ended. I now savored my DB Draught and Lion Brown, indicative of how I dove into this culture when the 1970s were later termed the 'beer-drinking dark age'.

> It's Friday night, and I'm a little worse for wear as I
> accompany my friend home. He sings in an inebriated
> state. His song has something to do with not wanting to

end up hanging in an alleyway. He stops and a neon sign above him blinks perfectly in time with his song. We linger as he serenades the stars and another fellow drunk, slumped in a doorway.

"The gas passes out the ass. Keep walking and talking. It will all end on the eighth day of the week. I am Mr. Hungry Pants. I run down the street to beat the heat. Listen to my feet. The truth lies beneath my shoes. The whisper in my ear is not fear. Keep walking, my dear. I won't hang in an alleyway, no way."

He finishes, and I ask him to explain, but he is unable. I surmise he cannot remember the details of his song. No doubt he warbled tunelessly whatever popped into his head.

"The words are not the point," he slurs. "You've got to keep going. Can't let 'em beat you. Keep walking, Ron. Yank, my friend, you've got to keep going."

I agree wholeheartedly, and "listen to my feet" becomes my eternal motto. Like The Who, I am "going mobile".

New Zealand, the heavy consumer of malted barley and hops for the nation's beers was also the land of fifteen million sheep, three million people, and countless dairy farms. After the brewery strike, the front-page news expressed concerns regarding a shortage of milk, purportedly leading to all Kiwis being forced to drink powdered milk within five years.

This headline, citing a recent research survey, created a tremendous uproar for a few days. The love of fresh milk was threatened, and some believed lamb might follow. After reading the latest situation before work one morning, I passed honeycomb tripe in the window of a butcher shop. First, it was a beer shortage. Would this ubiquitous organ be next?

The daily jaunt to work was part of my comfortable routine. I washed and drove cars to the airport before returning to the rental agency by bus. Tea and 'smoko' (a smoke break) were morning and afternoon rituals, full of lively employee banter. Before beer in the evenings, tea was the favored drink, and, despite missing coffee, I developed a taste for tea. I was firmly immersed in Kiwi culture.

Once a month, a group of Tasman workers, including the attractive girls behind the rental counter, accompanied us to the pub for a party. It was a festive time as we drank numerous pints of beer and sang choruses of *Roll out the Barrel*. It was a grand time to be in New Zealand, and during my eventual three months in Auckland, I did not meet any other American travelers. Maybe it was off-season? A few Canadians, along with Kiwis and the Aussies I met, constituted my circle of friends.

My buddies recommended Rotorua as a must-see destination, and a rental car with my staff discount was a perk. One of the options was a Mini Cooper S, and after seeing Michael Caine use these to great effect in his 1969 crime caper, *The Italian Job*, this influenced my choice. The 143-mile drive on the left side of the road to see this picturesque town would add an additional degree of adrenaline to the open road for the weekend.

The drive was primarily through the countryside, and there was light traffic on the roads. I maneuvered the little car, whipping around corners and accelerating in the straightaways. My flame for travel was rekindled with my expanding bank account.

The Rotorua name originates from Maori, with *roto* being lake, and *rua* meaning two. It was named after the second lake discovered by Maori Chief Ihenga in the 14th century, and today, it is one of many lakes found in the northeast of New Zealand's north island. The town lies inland from the coast, protected by high country to the south and east, resulting in less wind than in other areas in New Zealand.

The gorgeous sparkling lakes and striking lush forests provided a scenic backdrop for my getaway. The dramatic geysers and active hot mud pools were notable reminders of our planet's beauty. Propped by a sturdy tree, I gazed across a lake-filled caldera for several hours. Images of a diver slowly recovering from the bends in a decompression chamber were a mirage. The difference in my mind was a vision of my own slow decompression from the deep dives of darker events, and the hypnotic effect of nature worked its magic.

My next goal was Australia, and I submitted my work permit application at the Australian Embassy in Auckland. It was a logical step, and I prayed for a speedy acceptance. My intention was to work my way across the continent, visiting sights such as Ayers Rock, Sydney, and Darwin, and as many places in between as possible. In the interim, I soaped and polished cars with gusto, daydreaming of destinations after Australia. The typical backpacker route was from Darwin to Portuguese Timor before island hopping to Bali, Indonesia. From there, I envisioned traveling across Asia and on to Europe.

I pictured the adventurous nature of travel unleashing the invisible hands around my neck squeezing happiness from my soul. The power of karma leads the way, as the happy hippie traveler wanders the world. No doubts, no worries, only freedom as I crest the next hill, and another new road.

By the end of my second month in Auckland, I received unexpected and shocking news—my application for an Australian work permit was denied without explanation. My plans were abruptly derailed, and Australia was crossed off the list until my next world tour. I retired to the pub to be my cerebral self, and after several pints of DB Draught, I settled for Bali.

I frequented various travel agencies during my lunch hour as I hunted for airfares to Bali, Southeast Asian cities, and beyond as far as New Delhi. The 'per mile' airfares in the Pacific were the highest in the world, and the quoted prices were generally around $600.00 to $800.00 one way. As I left yet another office, I saw a poster advertising a cruise to Antarctica for $250.00. This was within my budget and sounded tempting. As I dashed back to work, I amused myself by visualizing hitchhiking through Antarctica with a penguin as my companion.

By the third month of my stay, I happened upon a well-versed travel agent, who described the practice of purchasing a flight to the furthest destination. The calculation was based on the miles to the most distant destination, allowing additional stopovers without increasing the overall cost. To my utmost delight, she said a flight from Auckland to Tel Aviv amounted to $340.00 with eight stopovers in Bali, Singapore, Saigon, Vientiane, Bangkok, Rangoon, Dhaka, and Bombay! Wow, my prayers were heard, and as I write these words now, this miraculous fare still astounds me.

One last evening with my pals, and it was a riotous night in the pub. They gave me a wild send off, and as I daydreamed on the bus to Auckland airport for my morning flight, I was flooded with mixed emotions. The level of difficulty in leaving good friends was always the same; it never decreased. Perhaps this is why "hello" and "goodbye" are the same word in many languages.

There were no nonstop flights from New Zealand to Denpasar, Bali's capital city, in those days. As the plane descended, my spirits were buoyed to see Sydney since there was a stopover before Bali. I was granted a transit visa for 24 hours until the next leg of my flight, and this was my chance to see some of this iconic city.

Through the window of the plane, I viewed a huge, white, unfinished cavernous structure soon to be dedicated as the Sydney Opera House. At the time, many Australians detested the appearance of this modern-looking building and considered it an ugly monstrosity. There was widespread controversy and "Too bad it couldn't be the Sydney Public House" was uttered by a few Aussies. Today, not only is the Sydney

Opera House a major architectural and cultural icon, it is undoubtedly the pride and joy of the city, attracting 8.2 million annual visitors from Australia and around the world.

For several hours, I reveled in the sights and sounds of Sydney, bustling with activity. New Zealand habits prevailed at dinnertime, and I visited a pub for fish and chips. As I sipped my beer, I checked out the 'birds' (aka girls) to see if one flew my way. In case you're curious, they flew in the opposite direction.

The disappointment of leaving Sydney in six hours instead of six months was disheartening. By evening, it was tempting to overstay my transit visa and work illegally. However, the fear of being arrested and deported again was unnerving. The risk versus reward tilted toward the airport for my flight to Bali.

TRACK TWENTY ONE

ELTON JOHN: CROCODILE ROCK

In New Zealand, the winds of destiny led to a secure job and a return to growing a savings account. My original strategy was to work for a month in New Zealand before traveling to Australia. It was through the backpacker grapevine I heard jobs in Australia were available for itinerant travelers. The direction changed, and I was in Bali sooner than expected.

I breezed through Immigration—with money in my pocket and an onward ticket to my next destination—and spotted a tourist kiosk in the airport terminal. I asked the lone attendant behind the counter the perfect question, "Where do the hippies go?" His all-knowing response was, "Kuta Beach, of course!"

I proceeded to the nearest group taxi which was a pickup truck with wooden benches on the bed. Almost all developing countries have these primitive means of transportation. In Haiti, they are called 'tap-taps' and in Colombia, they are 'chiva buses', etc. Twenty minutes later, in Kuta Beach, I located a small primitive inn with rooms for $2.00 per night. The five rooms of the inn were private, although toilets and bath were shared.

I adapted to showering Indonesian-style. There is no upward pipe with a shower head, but instead, a square concrete tub filled with cool water and a large pitcher hanging on the wall. The method entailed standing next to the tub, scooping water into the pitcher and then pouring it over myself. Once wet, I soaped my entire body and then rinsed several times by scooping and pouring. It was an archaic yet effective process. The temperature in Bali rarely falls below 82°F, equivalent to the temperature of the bath water.

My tiny room included a bed and chair, a welcome alternative to a bush, even a five-star one. I unpacked my few belongings when I heard a knock on the door. There was a stunning blonde-haired girl with a delicious smile named Libby, a librarian on holiday.

"Hi, I saw you come in. Fancy going for a swim?" she asked in a distinct Aussie accent.

What an auspicious start to my time in Kuta Beach!

"Sorry, I don't have a swimsuit," I replied.

She smiled seductively as she said, "You don't need one."

The beach was long and lovely, as was Libby, with a backdrop of mostly trees and tufted grass. It extended for miles in both northerly and southerly directions. Libby and I were alone on the beach, except for a few surfers seeking to catch the waves in the distance. Despite the agitation of the waves, the water was crystal clear.

The hot sand between my toes triggered recognition of the fact I had accomplished my eight-month journey crossing the Pacific Ocean. I visualized myself glum on the Monterey Pier, and now, here I was close to 9,000 miles away from California and the past.

The exhilaration coursed through my veins as I exploded with overwhelming joy, jumping up and down, my arms raised in uncontrollable exuberance as I launched skyward. My skin tingled, my heart raced, and my body was covered with goosebumps. The ecstatic joy and euphoria blasted my hat off my head. It was the greatest day ever, coupled with Libby as we frolicked in the ocean.

Today, Kuta Beach is the busiest town in Bali with a myriad of shops, bars, and restaurants attracting hundreds of thousands of visitors. In 1971, surf, sun, and fun were in their infancy, and it was a small fishing village consisting of one-story wood and concrete homes, many with thatched roofs. The unpaved streets and paths, lined with palm trees, connected one to the other, and all led to the undeveloped beach, devoid of hotels. Phones and electricity were scarce; kerosene lamps provided light.

A small crowd of fifty sunset spectators congregated on the sand near the only beachside bar and restaurant. A traditional, thatched open-air restaurant, the tables and chairs were conveniently arranged on the sand, a hundred feet from the soothing, incoming waves. It was peaceful with panoramic views for the upcoming sunset. This was Libby's recommendation, and I sipped a beer before nature's impending dazzling show, which promised to be a picture postcard moment.

The sun began its final descent for the day, and it was clear why the sunset was popular for tourists and locals in this part of the world. It was a natural kaleidoscope of endless colors and hues, featuring a hypnotic display for twenty minutes. The long-lasting duration of the sun's daily disappearance, combined with intense rainbow effects, produced a truly magical event.

Granted, sunsets were the easier choice, and I guessed the sunrises in Bali to be as magnificent as its sunsets. The consistent sunrise and sunset time in Bali does not vary by more than fifteen minutes year-round due to its 600-mile proximity to the equator. The beach at sunrise before the onset of scorching daytime temperatures would be a wise choice. The absence of shade and afternoon lingering was a surefire recipe for sunburn and dehydration.

The beachside restaurant was packed with other backpackers guzzling beer and regaling their latest antics. The atmosphere became raucous after sunset as we ordered dinner and more beer. On the main backpacker trail in Bali, people generally traveled to India and Europe, while others ended their journeys in Australia and New Zealand. This eclectic mix meant it was easy for people to find common ground and share experiences and travails of other popular destinations.

I also gleaned information from other travelers on local tourist attractions. The scuttlebutt was the only restaurant on the main thoroughfare that offered a 'special omelet' breakfast. This meal included toast, mangosteen, coffee, and the special omelet-$1.00 with magic mushrooms or 50 cents without.

The sights and sounds of the village intensified as I ventured home at 11:00 p.m. The atmosphere was festive, with locals dressed in ceremonial costumes and dancing to the incessant beat of drums. It was Mardi Gras in another dimension. Despite my immersion in the merriment and hullabaloo, an intriguing quandary was soon revealed.

In my hasty departure, distracted by a beautiful blonde, I had left without an address for the inn, and Libby was sound asleep. My recollection was a small, nondescript building. All the houses and palm trees blended at night into a maze of sameness. House numbers and street signs were few or non-existent, unnecessary for locals in a small village. Directions were given using landmarks such as palm trees or so and so's house.

I aimlessly followed a parade of exotic-costumed dancers for the second time and was the lost stranger in the middle of somewhere. My memory was jogged, recalling the inn was close to the main highway, and I headed in that direction to retrace my steps. Thirty minutes later, the familiar carved front door was a welcome sight.

It was an eventful day between the flight from Sydney, my new girlfriend, the memorable beach sunset, and an unfamiliar culture to absorb. As I closed my eyes in bed, the lesson was to obtain a business card or memorize the lodging address before going out on the town.

It was simpler to navigate the village in daylight. The casual dining restaurant recommended the previous night was 'downtown' between two palm trees. I use this term loosely because it was the only establishment on the main dirt road before the beach. The other diners ordered the special omelet and, feeling brazen, I ordered the same.

The restaurant seated approximately twenty people, sitting on each side of three picnic tables lined end to end. The accents indicated my fellow travelers were mostly from Australia. I was the lone Yank, and it was now three months since I had met another traveling American.

An Aussie guy across the table started with the usual "Where are you from?" and I answered, "Maryland, USA".

"Impossible! You're not a Yank!" he asserted with incredulous surprise. "I'm a seasoned traveler, and you can't fool me. You're an Aussie."

The debate ensued, and his insistence was insurmountable. I was baffled by what had become of my accent. Perhaps the months of discussions with my five Aussie friends finessed my accent with an Australian flair. The special omelet was served, and it was identical to a regular one; I paid my dollar and remembered to be cognizant of its peculiar "magic" ingredient.

After breakfast, I met Libby, and we meandered along the endless beach. There were a few people swimming or relaxing during our romantic walk. I suspected everyone in the village slept late because of the celebratory festival the previous night, but Libby explained only tourists went to the beach during the day. The locals visited the beach to bathe at night.

My mind was light, and my body was heavy. All aboard for the magical mystery tour. The shade under an alluring palm tree whispered, "Have a rest" as I reclined on the trunk and Libby continued her stroll. The space cadet daydreamed by the ocean, admiring the surf and sky while recalling the past eight months. The lifetime study of books, maps, and National Geographic magazines led to the passion of traveling around the world slowly becoming a reality. In the homestretch, life felt wondrous peering into the wild blue yonder. The space cadet toured the galaxy, far, far away on Kuta Beach.

The sun was high in the sky, and shade was diminishing. As the temperature rose, and the heat intensified, I envisioned a cool pina colada with a tiny umbrella in the glass. My first lesson with equatorial heat. Another hour or two was a prescription for dehydration and sunburn. The beach was deserted and understandably so.

Still reluctant to leave the shade, a mirage of a solitary figure surfaced in the distance, slowly moving in my direction. Every few steps the person stopped, bent over, and touched the sand before resuming. It was an unusual sight. The sandman inched closer. Was this a religious practice in Bali or was this a mushroom induced mirage?

A half hour elapsed before I introduced myself to the sandman, someone a few years older than me named Hans. He was from Amsterdam and clarified his obsession with the sand. Hans collected a specific shell for making necklaces. His objective was to gather 700 shells and the subsequent necklaces he sold in Dam Square financed his trip.

"I've done this many times, and I love it," he said, and I agreed it was a creative way to earn money by leisurely collecting seashells on his 'business trip'.

The effect of the mushrooms was lessening. My next stop was to quench my thirst and hunger back at the beachside restaurant where I saw my first Kuta Beach sunset. Hans and I ambled over there together, and

I discussed visiting his home city. He recollected the shoeshine boy in Dam Square, and we agreed it's a small world.

My ongoing celebration for crossing the Pacific next consisted of a cool pina colada with a tiny umbrella in the glass. The significance of the tiny umbrella is its representation of a tropical vacation. Hans and I were the afternoon's first patrons before others drifted inside to escape the heat. Beers were consumed, and stories flowed in this newly formed travelers' oasis. My suggestion that our job was to drink beer until sunset was greeted with hurrahs and much clinking of bottles and glasses.

The sunset viewing was the major daily event at the beachside restaurant, the preferred hangout for backpackers to share their recent activities. On the weekend, sunsets attracted more local spectators on motorbikes, including amorous couples catching the romance of the enchanting sunset. The days blended into a pleasurable routine as I deliberated the remainder of my Southeast Asia trip until the bump in the road surfaced.

On my first day in Kuta Beach, a tiny sliver of a thorn lodged itself squarely in the center of my right foot. It was not painful, and I merrily carried on until it was a growing nuisance. The village doctor's office hours were posted as "Open on Tuesdays and Fridays at 10:00 a.m.," and I visited on Tuesday, but apart from other would-be patients, no one else appeared. Friday also yielded no sign of life at the office. At this juncture, my concern escalated from casual to critical, and what was initially inconsequential was now urgent. It was arduous to walk a hundred yards without resting.

Festive blue and purple colors on the bottom of my foot radiated from the tiny thorn. Judging from the persistent, throbbing pain, the immediate concern was an infection. After a few more days, this fear was well-founded, and the infection coursing through my bloodstream was signaled by hallucinatory dreams.

I awake from a dream in the middle of the night. It is a warm night for a leisurely swim as I head towards the ocean one block away. I am naked as I walk the empty streets on the dirt path leading to the ocean.

The full moon illuminates the glistening water. I pause twenty feet from the surf to see a huge saltwater crocodile in a foot of water facing the shore. I freeze and stare into the crocodile's motionless eyes. Maybe he is asleep?

Three more crocodiles are in a row next to the first one. I turn and run, yelling "The crocodiles are coming! The crocodiles are coming!"

I shout warnings into the night air, and no one listens. My Paul Revere re-enactment is futile. I slumber, and now the crocodile is in my room, slowly munching on my foot.

The wisest option was to consult a doctor in Denpasar. After a thirty-minute truck taxi ride to the local hospital, I believed a simple remedy would resolve this foot problem.

The young lady at the admissions desk did not speak English, but I was able to pantomime my foot as the problem. She handed me a slip of paper with a room number on it. I was relieved to see a doctor shortly. In a cavernous room, standing next to an examination table, I heard one English word, "Sit". In the room were four other exam tables with patients surrounded by their families.

A big, brawny man advanced toward my table and pointed at my boots. I interpreted this gesture as a request to remove my boots and socks. Maybe he was the doctor. The minute my feet were bare, he disappeared.

Minutes later, a nurse came to my examination table and motioned for me to lie down. She examined my foot and waved to someone. Blind to the hand signals and the local language, I was unprepared for the remedy. The brawny man returned, now accompanied by three others of similar build. One man was stationed at each shoulder and one at each leg. Perhaps one of them spoke English?

"Sekarang," instructed the nurse, which I later understood meant 'now'.

At her command, all four men firmly held me in place as the nurse carved a large hole in the bottom of my foot. My definition of pain was forever redefined. It was going through the roof pain, past all the galaxies in the universe to the farthest point in the most distant universe to shake hands with infinity. My pain level chart was rewritten, becoming "ouch", "whoa", "I can't stand it" and "through the top of my head screaming and cursing as four men hold me in place!"

"Abses hampir gangren," advised the nurse as she applied a dressing and bandage.

The word 'hampir' meant almost, and I deciphered the rest. The Indonesian language is concise. The surgery amounted to cutting a ¾" inch circle, ½" deep on the bottom of my right foot ... without anesthesia.

After surgery, the nurse waved goodbye as I gingerly slid into my boots. I hopped out the door on one foot without the benefit of antibiotics, painkillers, or crutches. I resorted to using my hand to steady myself, using the wall as I hopped toward the exit. The slightest pressure on my foot sent shock waves of pain throughout my body to the point of losing the ability to focus my eyes.

The 300-foot hop to the front entrance with the aid of a wall was relatively easy. As I exited on one foot, the next hurdle was another 75 feet of unsupported hopping to board the waiting truck taxi. Other passengers on the benches was a sign of imminent departure, and they were enamored with my show and monitored my progress.

I wondered if someone might start betting on my progress. I was the champion hopper, moving uphill on an uneven, unpaved road, and at the halfway point, I became overconfident. I lost my balance and tumbled to the ground. The unsympathetic taxi passengers laughed as I regained my footing and resumed hopping, trying to ignore the throbbing pain.

The fact that the driver waited was the one highlight of the day. It was a bad day, and I don't recommend it. Leave 'hospital visit' off your itinerary. I hopped the two blocks from the truck taxi stop to my room and lay awake all night as the pain fluctuated between "whoa" and "I can't stand it" every few minutes. This was the pattern throughout the entire night.

This type of infection is common close to the equator, with heat being a factor, and going barefoot on the beach the original culprit. The dancing and prancing on the beach with Libby set the stage for the lone thorn hidden in the sand to enter my foot. I swore to never walk barefoot again. I wore my boots regardless of the ridiculous sight as the temperatures reached 110°F or 45°C in my later travels.

Ten days passed without improvement. I hired three local industrious children to deliver rice and noodles to my room. The good times were kaput, finished, over and out. The pain ruled the days, and my only entertainment was when the kids brought my meals and taught me the names such as mie goreng ayam for fried noodles with chicken. At other times, I read a book and did little else.

I burned through my travel funds and opted to leave Bali and fly to Singapore. My primary motivation was to find a doctor, preferably an English-speaking one. I was disappointed to leave Kuta Beach, my three little language teachers and Libby, who helped change my dressing. My main concern was to save my foot, and good times were placed on hold. After goodbyes, I boarded the plane.

In Singapore, it was problematic to locate a doctor until a pharmacy was recommended at my sixth stop. Directed to the rear of a pharmacy, the pharmacist examined my wound and advised, "Do not walk on your foot, or you will lose it." He prescribed a packet of antibiotics, the first medication since the surgery. A nearby hotel was my home, and a man-powered trishaw/bike taxi was my primary mode of transportation. The pain was a constant reminder to proceed slowly.

Forty-seven years after my surgery, my foot reacts with throbbing, pulsating pain today as I write this segment. The message is to never forget or my mind will send a jolt of physical pain. The lessons branded from physical and emotional pain of my early years are equally memorable, and both involuntarily expanded my mind. The choices of different paths or directions were impacted by excruciating pain, the loss of friends which attacked my core beliefs, and the shift of my injury which pushed my consciousness to higher levels. My molecules were forever altered.

I swapped my Balinese bed for a Singaporean one and prayed for improvement. The choices were to gamble walking for extended periods—and cause a permanent problem of taxi passengers forever laughing—or postpone the conclusion of my dream trip for another time. The throbbing pain and the squishing of my wound when I walked dictated the answer.

On the trishaw past Raffles Hotel, I was sorely tempted and asked the driver to stop. My lack of mobility prevented my entrance. The 75,000 or so nerve endings in my foot had the last word. I will order a Singapore Sling next time.

The troop strength in Vietnam was now less than 200,000 American troops, and a freelance job with one of the many American interests in Saigon was my next stop. The decision to postpone the remainder of my dream trip and miss the other six destinations was correct, yet heartbreaking.

Two weeks of slow recuperation further drained my savings. I did not possess a credit or debit card, a notion hard to fathom today. During those years, a credit card was virtually impossible to obtain without a credit history and employment. A traveler has options, and wise decisions are oftentimes crucial for survival.

The need to postpone my Southeast Asia tour was a misfortune which happens on the road. I will never know the outcome if my journey was not derailed. I missed historic events: In Saigon, there were election riots throughout the city. There was a revolution in Thailand. I missed the India-Pakistan war which led to the formation of Bangladesh. Months later, another traveler described his flight on the last plane from New Delhi as the India-Pakistan war raged. He said bombs exploded on the airport as the plane lifted off the runway. He recounted the terrifying experience with the thousand-mile look in his eyes. Perhaps my foot surgery saved me, as much as the nurse saved my foot.

TRACK TWENTY TWO
DAVID BOWIE: CHANGES

The savvy backpacker recognizes each country has something unique, and in the 1970s, Singapore was well-known as a place for inexpensive electronic gadgets. I purchased a new cassette tape recorder and a small Minox camera before my departure to Tel Aviv, popular items for the era to be sold or traded at another destination.

My foot had not improved since the surgery, and a trishaw was hired every day for transportation until I departed Singapore on November 2nd, 1971. The flight was smooth until an unexpected stop in New Delhi, India due to a bomb scare. The weary passengers congregated in the deserted terminal at midnight as the authorities combed the plane and luggage. After a two-hour investigation, a bomb was not uncovered, and we re-boarded the same plane. I trusted it was a thorough inspection and the plane landed safely at Lod airport in Tel Aviv, the second largest city in Israel after Jerusalem.

Located on the coast bordering the Mediterranean Sea, Tel Aviv was founded in 1909 by Jewish settlers on the outskirts of the ancient port city of Jaffa. The name translates as Spring Hill, although the hill was mostly sand. Immigration by predominantly Jewish refugees meant the growth of Tel Aviv soon outpaced that of Jaffa, which had a majority Arab population at the time. Tel Aviv and Jaffa later merged into a single municipality in 1950, two years after the establishment of the State of Israel.

My main objective was to locate a doctor upon landing. This was easier than in Singapore, and he examined my bandaged foot. The wound now had a defined miniature pouting mouth that squished as I walked. The doctor advised to keep the wound bandaged and to limit pressure on my foot. The importance of wearing protective footwear was reinforced. This hobbled traveler would have a healed foot a month later. My foot was saved, and this saga ended with a ginormous sense of relief.

A home was next on the agenda. At the kibbutz volunteer office, I was re-assigned to the same kibbutz near Haifa. I was uncertain a repeat was the right decision, as it defied my principle of new and different instead of tried and true.

On the bus to Haifa, some riders simultaneously smoked and munched on sunflower seeds, casually spitting the shells onto the floor; this was a practice unfamiliar to me. I was impressed by the dexterity of these smoking munchers.

The kibbutz had a wide range of volunteers from backpackers to college students on sabbatical to others attempting to ascertain the meaning of life. Each nationality had distinctive qualities, and it was an invaluable lesson in humanity to behold three Dutchmen assimilate within a few hours. They created a makeshift cafe in their room, inviting everyone who passed by for a cup of coffee. In several hours, they were acquainted with nearly all the volunteers—instant coffee, instant party, and instant friends. In a few weeks, not surprisingly, the three became proficient in Hebrew.

The work schedule was six days a week starting at 6:00 a.m. and ending at 12:00 p.m. My primary duty was driving a tractor. The five-minute training on the fundamentals of driving a utility tractor with its trailer hitch was the beginning of my love affair with these workhorses. I don't know the reason why except a tractor reminds me of a mighty oversized sports car, albeit a slow one.

Similar to a sports car driver, with a broad grin on my face, I drove the tractor throughout the grounds as I delivered supplies to the kitchen and provisions to the poultry houses and cow barns, etc. The other days, I worked in the cotton fields or in the orchards picking grapefruit and oranges. The training provided for assorted jobs was beneficial in developing a myriad of skills in a brief time. What seemed inconsequential then became indispensable building blocks in later endeavors.

In the afternoon, there was ample time to organize parties, and I became the entertainment ambassador. This entailed collecting money from my fellow volunteers, riding the bus to town four miles away, and returning with beer and snacks. My compensation was free beer and snacks. 1972 was welcomed with a bigger than usual New Year's Eve party.

The major news in January featured a Japanese cyclist traveling around the world on a unicycle, which was stolen in Jerusalem. A national recovery effort was mobilized, prompting the reappearance of his unicycle, and he proceeded on his journey. It is a unique perspective to tour the world, and I never heard if he succeeded.

A month later, a letter from Leo, my former Canadian roommate on the kibbutz, contained an interesting footnote. He was skiing in Zermatt, a famous ski and mountaineering resort in Switzerland and home of the Matterhorn. As Leo was sightseeing in town, a Japanese unicyclist rode by and remarked, "Bumpy roads here." The unicyclist news from Leo further illustrated the coincidences on the tourist trail. It was a gentle reminder to my dormant wanderlust.

My second time at this kibbutz was as rewarding as the first time. The volunteers changed on a regular basis, contributing to an ever-evolving stew of personalities. The parties and the camaraderie were nonstop. Nevertheless, I craved more, and after three months, my decision was to move to Jerusalem. The night before my departure, all the volunteers surprised me with a going away party and a wallet filled with money. It was an unforgettable and emotional send off for this entertainment ambassador.

Situated between the Mediterranean and the Dead Sea, Jerusalem is one of the oldest cities in the world, and by the mid-1970s, it exceeded Tel Aviv in population. The Old City in Jerusalem is divided into four quarters—Armenian, Christian, Jewish, and Muslim—and is home to the leading tourist sites in the world, including the Western Wall, the Church of the Holy Sepulcher, the Dome of the Rock, and more.

I rented a small apartment with a spacious open-air deck on Mt. Zion. The building was approximately 800 years old, constructed of large Jerusalem stone blocks. The exit door was at the edge of the deck and led to a stairway to the ground level. On the right was a doorway which was the entrance to the site of Jesus' Last Supper and King David's tomb was nearby. My apartment was originally designated for the caretaker of the Last Supper room when it was under Jordanian control.

On most days, my small, narrow stairway was deserted. Periodically, high-spirited tourists were on a mission to fulfill their lifelong dream to visit the Last Supper room. The stampede of incoming tourists blocked the exit to the steps, and I paused in the doorway for a few minutes. The hundred or so tourists trooped into my neighbor's place and sometimes, my emergence was greeted with awe.

It was hilarious when the tourists' expressions transformed into astonishment. These dazed, stomping tourists became overly animated as my door slowly opened, and a long-red-haired man peered from behind the door. As I stepped forward, many tourists soon had an enhanced Last Supper room experience; the second coming of Jesus was right in front of them! Their imaginations were led astray for a few hallucinating moments, and for me, it was an amusing way to start the day.

An intertwining link exists between foolish endeavors and death. A fool sees what he wants and believes nothing; this valuable lesson occurred one evening with my new friend Harvey. A hypnotic Quaalude—a strong sleeping pill—and a beer were our appetizers before dinner. It was a night to remember with Harvey as we became oblivious to the height of our intoxication.

At our favorite restaurant, the evening special was soup and salad. Harvey's love for soup hit a new level. In the classic way a drunkard lowers his head to the glass, Harvey hovered the spoon over the bowl as he slowly lowered his head into the soup ... and did not stop. He dove down until his face was immersed in the bowl, and this was the old comedy routine no one chooses to reenact in real life because it is not funny.

"It was a 'souper' rescue by me," I said to Harvey as I lifted his head. He laughed as he wiped his face with a napkin.

After dinner, we stumbled erratically in our stupor, unaware of our surroundings. Once the stares became evident, we headed to our favorite scenic lookout on Mt. Zion to avoid the crowd. Harvey identified the stairs with an "Ah ha" as he pointed, climbing the circular stairway to the top of a minaret which was open to the public.

It was a magnificent view at night, overlooking the old city and Mount of Olives. Millions of stars were above and two lone pedestrians below. The three-foot-high metal railing was a secure barrier to grasp for added stability. The eighty-foot drop to the stone pavement below seemed to be only eight feet from the ground at night. In my intoxication, my heavy head focused on the two pedestrians below.

Akin to Harvey's soup dive, I blacked out momentarily, and my hat drifted off my head. I lunged for my hat now twenty feet away from my outstretched arm with no concept of my whereabouts. In an effort to retrieve my hat, I was upside down, headed towards the pavement. With a fierce tug around my waist, Harvey yanked the back of my pants and pulled me upright as I regained my balance. My knee jerk reaction to grab my hat almost ended my life. Luckily, Harvey had the wherewithal to save my life.

Harvey was furious with my nonchalant reaction to the seriousness of what occurred. I suggested he use the word 'gravity' and he was not amused. I shrugged, and we tottered down the stairs for my hat. We ended the evening before it ended us.

The next morning, Harvey reiterated in detail how close I came to falling to my death because I did not fully comprehend the circumstances of the preceding night. Harvey's slow dive into his soup was safer than my slow dive towards the hard pavement. I agreed with Harvey to not mix gravity and drugs, and he appreciated the pun in my earlier comment.

Fast forward one year later in New York City, where I heard Harvey's tragic news through a mutual friend. On his way to work one day, Harvey slipped and fell down a flight of stairs at the subway entrance. He landed on his head and subsequently died. The manner of his death was incomprehensible. Typically, when a young man falls, he breaks a leg. When an old man falls, there is a greater probability of death. Sadly, I was not there to save Harvey's life. His death was inconceivable to me then and now. I was overwhelmed with grief.

Once the daily influx of tourists finished their sightseeing, all was quiet in my room. It had many of the same features when it was built 800 years ago, including candles for light. The laws of nature somehow were reversed one night. It was one of those incomprehensible occurrences, where a simple act becomes unfathomably difficult.

It was a warm Jerusalem evening as I became drowsy after reading. The candle was next to my bed to be easily extinguished, and I leaned close to give it a hearty puff of air. With the flame extinguished, and my head on the pillow, I was engulfed in darkness when suddenly the candle re-ignited on its own. Perhaps a lingering spark on the wick was the cause? I blew on the candle with a stronger breath, and the flame was extinguished again. There were no hidden sparks on the wick, and none were visible in my dark room.

This time, although anxious to rest, I intently monitored the candle. Three seconds later, the flame re-lit itself and burned brightly. Now I was intrigued and baffled. With my mouth an inch away from the candle, I blew the mightiest gust of air and the flame extinguished. I felt victorious when the extinguished candle remained unlit in the darkness for five seconds. I reclined onto my pillow and closed my eyes, content to fall asleep when the candle re-lit itself!

Now it felt spooky, easier to explain if I was stoned, and I cautiously peered around the room. It was empty, except for me. I blew out the candle for a fourth time, and it finally remained unlit as I laid back on my pillow. What had transpired was beyond comprehension, and it left me with an eerie feeling that I was not alone in the room. I did not have an answer for this phenomenon, and since it was not accompanied by a thunderbolt, I nervously slumbered.

I awoke in the morning, energized by the candle incident, and bolted out of my room in search of an answer. My friends who lived nearby said nothing unusual occurred in their room last night. They were puzzled by my question. Over the following nights, the candle extinguished effortlessly after the first puff of air. The inexplicable happens.

One of my daily routines was a 15-minute walk for breakfast at my favorite brick oven bakery in the old city market. I ordered a breakfast quiche and Turkish coffee. This bakery was a secret hideaway, comprised of a single table and four chairs. It was a bread bakery until 9:00 a.m. in the morning when the baker served breakfast quiches to walk-in customers for an hour before closing. This was my introduction to brick oven cooking, and the pleasure blossomed to building my own wood-fired brick oven in the future.

The countless visits to the market were always different. There was an ongoing cacophony and activity among the masses of beckoning shop owners, energetic tourists, and impatient delivery men. This was people watching at its finest, as I was presented with an entertaining live show in this bazaar every day.

The shops sold souvenirs, tea, coffee, spices, pastries, and hookahs. An eclectic mix of people ranged from merchants to religious pilgrims to backgammon players. This lively marketplace was a magnet, where tourists and locals paraded nonstop. The sights, smells, and sounds emanating from the bustling, narrow streets have not changed in thousands of years.

The souvenir shop merchants unlocked and opened the rolling security doors and displayed colorful clothing, jewelry, and accessories. The delivery men pushed their overflowing wagons filled with goods through the streets into the market. Vendors busily filled their food stalls, stocking figs, dates, pomegranates, and melons, along with cucumbers, squash, hot peppers, and tomatoes.

After breakfast, I began the day at the busiest tourist entrance, Jaffa Gate, one of the main gates leading into the old city. This was the location for my private tour guide services, primarily to pretty girls. It was a winning formula for me and my tour guide groupies.

The lure of kibbutz life was irresistible after six months in Jerusalem. I landed on Kibbutz Sasa in northern Israel near the Lebanese border. The peace and quiet were a pleasant change from city life, and my new duties included harvesting carp from the fish ponds and picking apples in the orchard. I resumed my unofficial role as entertainment ambassador.

All amenities were provided, ranging from room and board to laundry and sewing. My major purchase was a waterbed from Megan, a departing volunteer headed to Dublin. The sales pitch was lovemaking on a waterbed was superior compared to a traditional bed. Several girls wished to test this theory. Frequently, I slipped into bed and discovered a willing participant. Other times, girls visited while I was asleep, and it wasn't a dream.

On New Year's Day morning, the sounds of exploding bombs interrupted my slumber. Half-asleep, I recognized the bombs were in the distance, and I snoozed for another hour. For good or bad, my attitude towards bombs and bullets was nonchalant, akin to a seasoned soldier. The news during breakfast was a rocket exploded on a nearby field, and the Air Force retaliated. It was a constant reminder of the fragility of life.

The roulette wheel of life spun and landed on Tel Aviv, where I completed paperwork for extending my visa. A convenient place to sleep was a cemetery near the beach and public showers. As I dozed, the lights of the Hilton hotel were a quarter of a mile away, and I coveted its trappings—a comfortable bed, climate-control, room service, and other luxuries.

As I recalled how the Icelandic prop-plane set a new baseline for flying, the Hilton hotel was a future goal for lodging. The luxury hotels and amenities would be a part of my next world tour. My dreams of becoming an upmarket traveler were for another day. The hardships I overcame as a budget backpacker were an Ivy League education. I applied this knowledge to business and personal relationships throughout my life.

The fine tuning of ingenuity simply occurs. There are many budget-friendly options for eating and showering. There is generally at least one inexpensive menu item for a filling meal, usually the local specialty or a lunch special. The search for a shower presented a bigger challenge, but typically I showered in athletic clubs, hostels, YMCA branches, truck stops, on the beach or preferably, in a new girlfriend's hotel room.

In my hungriest times, leftover bread at an outdoor sidewalk café table beckoned. Generally, pretty girls came to my rescue. My usual overture when I saw an attractive maiden was to ask, "How would you like to make a hippie happy?" The female knights in shining armor responded with money, food, or a place to sleep.

On Banana Beach in Tel Aviv, I met curvaceous Cindy, splashing and giggling in the surf. It was the first day of her college vacation, and before long we were licking ice cream cones topped with date syrup and pistachios. In our good humor and ice cream state of mind, a casting agent hiring movie extras advanced towards us. An opportunity for easy money was answered with our split second "Yes." He instructed us to be at the airport at 9:00 a.m. the next morning for filming.

The movie was an action spy adventure called *The Execution* starring Jason Robards. While the film was made in 1973, it wasn't released in the U.S. until 1976, likely due to Jason Robards' high profile in connection with his Oscar winning role in *All the President's Men*. In the film, he played an Israeli anti-terrorist officer, and it was in this cinematic offering that eleven-year-old Jennifer Jason Leigh made her debut in a non-speaking part. She was the 'girl with a rubber ball' and her face was never seen.

Our first scene was as Jason Robards cleared Immigration with Cindy next in line. Twenty-five feet beyond, I removed my coat, marking my acting debut. This scene was re-shot 25 times since Jason Robards was hungover from the previous night. In another scene, I exited the airplane with other 'passengers' onto the boarding ramp. Life as a movie extra is generally boring, but the bountiful buffet of food was a break from the monotony as we killed time until the next scene.

Despite the tedious aspects of being a movie extra, it was a cushy job. My next gig was *Jesus Christ Superstar*, where I was in various crowd scenes. These two movie appearances marked the foray into my short-lived show business career.

With an extended visa, I headed to the resort town of Eilat, located on the Red Sea at the southernmost tip of Israel. With its remarkable views of Jordan, it is famed for its beaches, coral reefs, nightlife, and desert setting, all contributing to a popular destination for domestic and international tourists. This was my next home for several months.

The daytime temperatures in Eilat were typical desert weather, averaging 110°F with 10% humidity. My next profession was longshoreman, also known as stevedore. It was a big improvement from the docks of Rotterdam. Loading and unloading cargo ships was a superior job than cleaning their holds at night, but nonetheless falling ill-distributed cargo was hazardous. For anyone not paying attention, instant death was a possibility. The danger of being crushed by falling cargo in Eilat versus falling from scaffolding in Rotterdam. Agility was the key to avoid injury. Ships and boats have an added element of danger; it's the nature of the (sea) beast.

In my spare time, I skin dived in turquoise blue waters, swimming with dolphins and tropical fish along the coral reefs. One of my odd jobs was selling popsicles to sunbathers on the beach. I purchased two dozen popsicles in their original cardboard box racing to sell them before they melted in ten minutes. In hindsight, the absence of a cooler was a hindrance. Nevertheless, selling from the cardboard box was a way to hone my sales ability; a method to earn money despite the heat and time constraint.

Eventually, I headed home and booked a flight to New York City.

> *We all associate places with memories … and memories with places. Yes, I had good times as well as bad, and why would I want to go home? I see a future there, but what did the future offer? Like Scrooge in A Christmas Carol, could the 'yet to come' erase the past? Was too much embedded in my psyche?*

> *Questions, questions, questions. Or is it equations? Travel + discovery = joy. Past + home = x. Define x and write your answer.*

> *Travel has changed me, and my experiences have taught me. Does going back 'there' offer the chance to look forward?*

Backwards - forwards. Forwards - backwards. What new change and new direction can I expect?

I have been away two years and three days and today is February 11th, 1973. It is upsetting to prematurely end the journey, but I am intent on confronting the anxiety. The line in the sand has been drawn, and I am homeward bound.

It was on a wing and a prayer that I chose wisely. My warped view in retrospection envisioned a rosy future. As the plane flew closer to New York, the bubbling inner turmoil swirled in a delirious state to the extent that my nervousness was visible to a vigilant sky marshal, and the plane was diverted to Montreal for a security check. The airline industry was justifiably cautious after thirteen hijackings in 1972.

All the passengers deplaned into the airport terminal while the plane was searched. One hour later, we re-boarded, and my seat area was in disarray. The sky marshal erred on the side of caution for the safety of the passengers, and I now concealed my discomfort.

Safely landing in New York, as I exited the plane, the sky marshal asked, "How are you?" in Arabic. I responded in kind since I understood simple Arabic from when I lived in the old city of Jerusalem.

TRACK TWENTY THREE

JETHRO TULL: LIVING IN THE PAST

On the bus from JFK airport to the city of Elizabeth in New Jersey, it was wiser to hitch a ride to the NJ Turnpike and on to Maryland. My preference was a slower re-entry into Bowie as I resumed being the American hippie hitchhiker on home soil, thumb outstretched for a driver willing to stop.

My seat was at the back of the bus as it traveled westward. I was energized by the prospect of hitchhiking on the edge of the highway once more, imagining who I'd meet. The deluge of memories from the last four years erupted in my mind; the same as a jigsaw puzzle with all the disparate pieces soon-to-be interlocked. My stream of consciousness flowed towards retrospection after having had a lifetime of adventures.

Out the window, I sought the familiar, not the new. This was 'home' and not a new inspiring foreign land. I was fine until the Outerbridge Crossing, a cantilever bridge which spans the Arthur Kill between Staten Island and New Jersey.

There were ships and docks, and for a moment, I longed to be in Israel and Rotterdam. My head snapped to see the seat in front of me; it didn't resemble something on an airplane.

I asked the driver for directions to the turnpike, and exited the bus, popping into a convenience store for snacks. The country underwent dramatic price inflation during my absence. This was the first rude awakening of my re-acclimation. It was after 11:00 a.m., and while my body clock said otherwise, it was irrelevant what meal was next.

My tiny backpack survived the journey, including the coat from Lionel. I was grateful for it as I turned up the collar. It was a crisp morning, with weak sunshine attempting to break through the clouds. A few gulls squawked overhead as they scanned for food from above.

I marched to the highway from the bus stop within minutes, devouring two Hershey Bars along the way. They were a perennial favorite before my travels, and their familiar flavor on my taste buds was a pleasant reminder of home. I convinced myself this was a good sign. Counting cars and trucks, it was the 34th vehicle which stopped. I trotted along the shoulder towards a light blue Ford station wagon with anti-war stickers on the fender and back window.

"Hello young man. Where are you headed?" asked a spritely older lady after I opened the door. She was perhaps in her mid-60s and, with pure white curls and a beaming smile, I imagined her as an actress on TV commercials as the consummate grandma.

"I'm going to Bowie, Maryland ma'am."

"Get in, it's your lucky day. I'm going to Baltimore to visit my daughter."

It was warm in the car, yet she wore a heavy red overcoat; with her hair color, she resembled a female Santa Claus. She was a live wire, and Lettie—as she insisted I call her—said her granddaughter was due to start kindergarten in the fall. The unfortunate part was her son-in-law was a POW in Vietnam. Several days later, I read in the newspaper that Operation Homecoming had begun, with a target of bringing almost 600 POWs home from Hanoi. I hoped Lettie's son-in-law was one of them.

Lettie was Jewish and was inquisitive on my perspective on the Middle East. She hoped the impending visit of Israeli Prime Minister Golda Meir, for meetings with Richard Nixon and Henry Kissinger, would result in peace and stability. Her reference was to when President Sadat of Egypt expelled Soviet advisers from Egypt the previous year and signaled to Washington his willingness to negotiate.

"What are you going to do now that you're back, Ron?" she asked with a glance to her right. "I expect your family will be pleased to see you?"

I glanced out the window, pausing a few moments before I answered.

"I'm not sure ma'am ... Lettie. Maybe I'll stay a while in Bowie and then return to New York."

"And your family?" she urged, as I heard the raise of her eyebrows in her voice. It was clear family matters were important to her.

"Oh, it will be good to see them," was the non-committal answer which earned another sideways glance. She began speaking and then noticed my expression. I gazed out the window and hoped I did not appear rude. There was no point in delving into my family dynamics.

Before I left Bowie two years ago, my parents had separated. I started my journey with a note on the kitchen table stating I'd be back in two weeks. I wrote to my family often as I traveled onward. Letters from home were infrequent because I was on the move. This meant I was unaware of news from my family. Based on my family's history, I was potentially entering an alternative reality.

The conversation with Lettie shifted to more mundane matters, in addition to touching upon some of my travel exploits. She visited Europe, including Amsterdam, several years earlier, and we had common ground in mutually visited places.

"I'll shine your shoes," I offered, and she laughed heartily.

Lettie brought sandwiches which she insisted on sharing with me, and it was approximately three hours later when she pulled over near a bus stop in Baltimore. I thanked her for the ride, and I had almost closed the door when she spoke her parting words.

"And Ron ..." I bent down to look at her. "I'm sorry if things are not great in your family, but I wish you happiness. Don't worry; you'll find it. And you will travel in the future."

I was startled by her perceptiveness, and before I responded, she smiled and gave another brief chuckle.

"Don't worry. I was a psychologist!" she said. I laughed and closed the door. Lettie was another character to add to my list of fond memories.

An hour later, my mother opened her front door.

"Hi Mom," I said as she recovered from the shock of my return.

"Oh, you're back. Come in," she replied as she led the way into her house.

The living room was decorated with the same paintings, and as I passed the living room doorway, there was my painting of the hobo. She moved it from my bedroom, and perhaps she thought I'd never return. In the kitchen, she sat at the table with the coffee she'd been drinking.

"How have you been, Mom?" I asked as I poured coffee from the pot on the stove.

"I'm fine. What are your plans? How long are you staying?" she asked.

"I don't know. I'll visit with a few friends and then probably go to New York."

It was three weeks before I went to New York. Although I wasn't in my mother's house, often it was tiring to observe her behavior, the consummate actress. I was wary as to what lay beneath her charade of congeniality.

Within hours, I was out the door to see old friends and first was Tulip. We were attracted to one another but not romantically compatible, so we remained friends. Tulip sent several letters during my travels with the latest Bowie updates.

Tulip had moved, and there were other changes in her life. At her new home, she opened the door, and I couldn't believe my eyes. Gone was the wild long hair, flowing skirts, and masses of beads, replaced with shorter hair, tied in a ponytail, jeans, and a white shirt. Her make-up was softer, with eyes sparkling beneath barely colored eyelids.

"Ron? My God! It is you!" she squealed and launched herself at me for a hug reminiscent of the old days.

"I can't believe you're here," she said as we stepped apart. Now there were a few tears in her eyes and a lump in my throat. Homecoming was hard.

"How are you?" she asked, brushing embarrassingly at her cheeks. "It was a year since I received a letter. Oh, this is far out! Come on in, it's cold."

She ushered me into her kitchen, and there was her son. A little boy with a broad smile sat in a high chair attempting to eat a cookie. He looked at me and burst into giggles.

"Say hello to your Uncle Ron, Oliver," Tulip said as she picked up her son, ignoring the soggy crumbs smearing the shoulder of her shirt.

Tulip had married my friend Greg and worked as a part-time secretary in an elementary school while in college. Still self-assured and self-confident, this was the girl who professed as a teenager she wanted to become a rock star like Janis Joplin. Tulip had become more mature and conservative, that's for sure.

I joined Tulip and Greg for dinner a few days later. One of the dinner conversation topics was the latest trends. The mainstay white T-shirts were no longer in vogue, replaced by printed ones with corporate and brand names. This new fashion statement was unknown to me. I was puzzled and asked if wearers were paid to advertise for these companies.

Tulip and Greg were the initial catalysts for the bombardment of changes I witnessed. It was difficult to process they were married and had a child. It was surreal to be home, and the reconnection with friends and family was staggering. My adventures altered my outlook forever. I was home, and it was foreign.

> *There are huge contradictions to reconnecting with old friends. In some ways, we've never been apart, and then there's the reality that our lives have changed.*
>
> *No matter the gap, no matter the new circumstances, we're the same people inside who were young and carefree. (Now I sound old.)*
>
> *How do I adjust?*
>
> *Hug me and tell me you care. I'm sorry I didn't write often, it doesn't mean I wasn't thinking of you. Out of sight means out of mind. Is that right?*
>
> *Did we drift apart? That's what lovers do.*
>
> *Remember the time when ... What about ... Can you believe we ... Are you sure we went? Oh no, what he said was ... It was when she wore her ...*
>
> *It's been good to see you. We must keep in touch. I promise I'll write. I will.*

It was the status quo with my parents. Despite the separation, my parents still squabbled and behaved irrationally toward each other. As usual, I was the parent, helping two bickering kids behave and their attitudes, bordering on insanity at times, drove me to distraction. Finally, I was at my limit. I said goodbye and headed to the greener grass of New York for a new conventional life. My intrepid backpacker lifestyle, overflowing with adventure, was on hold.

TRACK TWENTY FOUR

THE BEATLES: MAXWELL'S SILVER HAMMER

The adjustment to a sedentary lifestyle was grueling. My carefree backpacker existence filled with adventure was replaced by a job as a travel agent at the AAA (American Automobile Association). As B.B. King sang of the thrill being gone, I regretted my decision.

Perhaps with the intent of boosting my flagging spirits, one evening my pal Al suggested we go clubbing, and he acted as my guide for the Upper East Side nightclub scene. We ventured to the Blue Water Club to drink and carouse.

Always the opportunist, near the entrance, Al instantly approached a girl close to a group of teenage boys and introduced himself. The gist of their conversation was Dora, as she introduced herself, said she did not have her identification to enter the club. She solicited our help to bypass the doorman. We strode inside as Dora beamed and hugged Al.

After a round of drinks, Dora proposed another club and Al agreed, smitten by this petite, lively blonde with an ample chest and a button nose. Upon exiting, she taunted the same group of teenagers on the sidewalk.

"See you, boys. I'm leaving with real men!" Dora bragged. It seemed they were previously unsuccessful in wooing her.

While we waited for the walk sign to illuminate to cross the street, their reaction was swift. Over my right shoulder, I noted the eight boys, their honor tarnished, charge towards us wielding steel rods. I darted into First Avenue, which traverses north to south in Manhattan, and they were in hot pursuit.

Four teenage ruffians jumped Al, and the other four attacked me. All of them were hell-bent on remodeling our heads with the hefty-looking metal bars. I struggled to cross the road and evade them in traffic, and the blaring horn of a yellow cab forced me to jump back. I was cornered.

I was immediately pummeled to the ground in the middle of the avenue. The attack was not my only problem. I laid on the road in danger of being squashed as cars swerved around us, their horns blaring.

The onslaught by four bruised teenage egos progressed, and they clobbered me as the next wave of cars flowed with the green light. From the corner of my eye, I saw a driver exit his vehicle and fire his handgun into the air. The loud shot, like an athletic starting pistol, triggered the end of the assault, and the young thugs ran for their lives. After I loosely waved a battered arm in his direction, the man with the gun disappeared as I limped onto the sidewalk.

As I slowly regained my composure, Dora also vanished without a word. Al limped towards me bruised and bloodied.

"Shit, man. Are you okay?" he mumbled through split and swollen lips. He lost two teeth.

"I've been better," I replied, wiping the blood off my face. One blow cut the skin above my eyebrow. I ached all over, and my head throbbed the most.

The first witnesses to the attack were two middle-aged sisters in front of their apartment building. They kindly escorted Al and I upstairs, where they tended to our wounds. In their apartment, I recalled the times when my friends and family preached the dangers of foreign travel. The irony was not lost on me.

While I was envious at times of the clients I served at AAA, my job kept me close to the idea of travel. There were minor employee perks for traveling in the U.S. and Canada over the coming months. My travel agent status yielded a $20.00 weekend jaunt to the Palmer House in Chicago plus another weekend at the Queen Elizabeth hotel in Montreal.

With money in my pocket, an advertisement for a room in a shared apartment sent me to 69th Street in the Woodside neighborhood of Queens and conveniently located near the subway. Early one Sunday morning, I hopped on the #7 Flushing line to meet my potential roommates, Berat from Turkey, and Luciana from Colombia.

It was a three-bedroom, modern apartment nearly 800 years younger than my apartment in Jerusalem. They welcomed me as a roommate. Berat eventually showed me the rudiments of knife throwing, while Luciana shared the highlights of Colombia. Her friendship influenced my business decision eighteen years later to import emeralds from Colombia.

After Al and I recovered from the attack—mentally and physically— we resumed the social scene, including the Blue Water Club. We also frequented a dive bar called Hilly's in the East Village. By the end of the year, this bar closed following noise complaints from the neighbors. The owner, Hilly Kristal, later opened CBGB in the Bowery which became famed in the punk era for showcasing bands such as *Blondie* and *The Ramones*.

At a corner table in Hilly's, Al and I bantered who had the best voice, Robert Plant or Ian Gillan. A girl nearby interrupted and remarked the answer was Roger Daltrey. Al was adamant it was Gillan, and I said her choice was a close second to Robert Plant. Al wandered off and the girl, whose name was Judy, and I became acquainted.

With thick brown curly hair which cascaded over her shoulders and around her narrow face, she reminded me of Grace Slick, the singer from Jefferson Airplane who I admired at Woodstock.

"So, have you seen Led Zeppelin?" she asked, and I nodded as I finished my beer.

"Several times," I replied. "Have you seen The Who?"

We began exchanging stories of concerts and festivals, and she shyly blushed at my flirtatious comments. As the waitress placed two beers on the table, Judy slid her chair closer to mine. Judy discussed her job regarding a banking innovation—the first generation of ATMs—programming and implementing these machines in bank branches. I said my job was a former electronics genius from Stanford.

"Wow! How long have you been doing that?"

"Oh, half an hour," I replied, and she had the expected puzzled look.

"What do you mean?"

"I was in California and became a designated genius."

"But you said half an hour ..."

I explained the circumstances which led to the topic of travel, elevating my position to beyond genius. Her limited travel left her yearning for more. The evening passed as I entertained her with my exploits. She was skeptical about my foot, so I removed my boot and sock.

"Oooh, yuck!" she declared and then shuddered. "That must have really hurt?"

"Oh, it was just a scratch," I replied, and she hit my arm as she said, "Bah." I leaned forward to kiss her. It was a good night.

The fun times with Judy were a distraction for a few months. Our time together mostly comprised of dining at popular restaurants, seeing Broadway shows and movies, and eating homemade chocolate mousse in her apartment. Besides her good looks and pleasant nature, Judy was smart, cultured, and refined but slightly neurotic.

On May 5th, we attended the J. Geils Band concert together at the city's Academy of Music. Although famed for the 1980s pop hit *Centerfold*, the band had been born fifteen years earlier. The concert we attended was less than a month after the quintet released their third studio album, *Bloodshot*, which eventually reached #10 on the Billboard Pop Album charts.

In the summer of 1973, my latest stab at cultural assimilation into 'ordinary life' was the purchase of a new 10-speed bicycle in Manhattan. The simplest method was to pedal my new acquisition home to 69th Street across the Queensboro/59th Street Bridge or transport it on the subway. I chose the former option although bicycle lanes did not exist on the bridge.

The drive across the toll-free bridge by car lasts a few minutes, so why not ride the bicycle? I intended to cycle in the far-right lane, among the slowest vehicles. With views of the East River, Manhattan, Queens, and a hint of Brooklyn, the roadway was separated by a low barrier from the other two express lanes headed in the direction of Queens. This was my foolproof plan.

I was the one and only bicycle rider, boldly pedaling onto the bridge, and my ascent was slow and steady. The level of difficulty in pedaling uphill on a bridge, coupled with a line of impatient drivers behind me, was trickier than I surmised. Barely halfway to the top of the bridge, I realized my mistake. A U-turn guaranteed severe injury or death because of the roadway's narrow width filled with cars. I was unwittingly committed to success or catastrophe.

Some five years later, on the TV show *Taxi*, the Checker yellow cab gracefully cruised across the Queensboro Bridge to a catchy theme song. My view and experience were the opposite. While I struggled toward the pinnacle of the roadway with increasing exhaustion, my focus was on the second half of the ride, coasting downhill into Queens.

I crested the top to see the downhill portion of the ride was devoid of cars. With a deep breath, I coasted, hurtling down the empty roadway like a madman. It was critical to maintain balance on the checkered roadway, with its tiny notches of jagged steel, designed to shed water and ice into the East River. Falling meant being shredded like cheese on a grater. These gruesome thoughts stifled my breathing, and the difficulty increased dramatically to death-defying proportions.

This was not the smooth asphalt roads of Bowie; this was the monster of all roads to eternity. If my chances of survival on the uphill segment were poor, now careening down the other side, they were disastrous. At speeds beyond 40 mph, the bicycle was out of control, and from my childhood days, every biker knows that applying uneven pressure on the brakes spells disaster. I was one blink away from calamity and my demise; a new degree of terror emerged, never to be forgotten. This fiasco, in my mind, released a lifetime's worth of adrenaline.

The good news was the previously impatient drivers weren't upset, and they were cruising into Queens behind me. It was advantageous that fear had a seat on this ride since it added stability in maintaining my speed without crashing. I am astounded my tires and I survived.

My skill as a newspaper boy was a key part of my deliverance to the other side of the bridge. At the age of 13, with 50 or more newspapers in a basket perched above the front wheel, my route consisted of pedaling the hills of Bowie. I tossed banded newspapers on to every driveway with both hands—one left and one right—as I balanced the bicycle with my weight while speeding nonstop down steep hills. Today, there is a distinctly safer bicycle and pedestrian path to cross the Queensboro Bridge.

My next brush with death came only two weeks later. In broad daylight, with a full belly from lunch at the Blarney Stone Pub, I lingered for the Walk/Don't Walk sign at the junction of 7th Avenue and 33rd Street in Manhattan with other pedestrians. Lost in thought, a young man advanced from behind with his right hand in his coat pocket. I heard his brusque voice in my ear and hot breath on the back of my neck.

"I have a gun. Give me your wallet," he demanded.

Over my shoulder, I evaluated his youthful eyes and saw both menace and fear. Was I being confronted by a seasoned criminal intent on robbing a pedestrian on a crowded street corner?

It was a short run for him into the subway system. He had options, and I had one. Do I give this young boy my money? This dissolved into my complying or not to his demand. The walk sign illuminated, and this was my sign. I gambled it was a lame bluff. I cautiously crossed the street and went back to the office.

My first few months in the U.S. were similar to a wild lion in a zoo, confined to a small space. I missed the freedom, happiness, excitement, and camaraderie among other travelers. However, visiting Tulip and other friends contented with their lives meant my own future was questioned. My job description was nothing other than a hippie backpacker.

In my world travels, there was an abundance of exceptional products which were commonplace at their point of origin and inexpensive. This was the source for eventually pursuing an import/export business. The formula of Hans, the Dutch shell collector in Bali, was a reminder of the power of a simple business plan.

231

As I cycled to Al's one Saturday afternoon, the seed was planted to be self-employed, single, and travel the world buying products to sell. It was a dream for now, and the idea of remaining in the U.S. became more palatable.

> *I study my passport. There is one year left and then I'll renew it. Will I get it when it's time? Will I be ready to travel by then?*
>
> *So many stamps - so many places. Entries - Departures. Entries - Departures. Will every page of my new passport be filled with visas again?*
>
> *It is time to move forward in different ways. It's time to wait, time to reflect, time to accept what was cannot always be what will be.*
>
> *Wait a while and hit the pause button of life. Let someone else's wheels go around.*
>
> *How old are you now? I'm 23. There's still time.*
>
> *I look into the mirror, and what do I see? I'm older than the photo in the passport. I'm still young. There's still time.*
>
> *Now I'm repeating myself. Who am I trying to convince?*
>
> *Enough. This is it. Decision made.*
>
> *"See you later, passport," I say as I close the drawer. I eye my reflection in the mirror. And wink.*

PARTING SONG

LOUIS ARMSTRONG: WHAT A WONDERFUL WORLD

I rish novelist, playwright, and poet Oliver Goldsmith died in 1774, almost 200 years before my return from Israel, and I remember his quote:

"Life is a journey that must be traveled no matter how bad the roads and accommodations."

As a teenager, this was my rallying cry to travel. Years later, I recognized it was confronting the vagaries of life and maintaining momentum towards my dream. Travel became my life's mission-to tour the world firsthand.

It is preferable for some to choose a sedentary lifestyle, rarely straying from their birthplace. The old expression of the greater the risk, the greater the reward is also true on a personal level. It is difficult to fully comprehend the world from the comfort of one's living room. Strangers all over the world were benevolent and welcoming. I was often treated as a family member in seconds. In a way, it sounds magical; these are the mind-boggling, incomprehensible levels of hospitality which arise when traveling and are generally absent in the daily routine of life.

As I approach my 70th year, my love for traveling has not diminished. This year—when this first volume of travel adventures is completed—I visited Canada, England, Belgium, Germany, the Czech Republic, Poland, the Netherlands, Israel, the Dominican Republic, Barbados, St. Lucia, and St. Kitts.

The joys of travel encompass witnessing the wonders of the world with the bonus of expanding one's perspective. All countries possess at least one specialty and being at the source is invaluable. If an area perfected a craft for hundreds or more years, such as beer in Germany, it was my aim to indulge in the best of the best.

There are many variances and finite degrees which push the limits of perfection. This involves centuries of evolution for a craft to achieve excellence in a competitive field. To admire the highest level of craftsmanship is to gain wisdom. These are the little things that matter, those which add to the composite experience of travel. It is the overall definition of a country which is its true representation.

As much as inhabitants are unique from country to country, overall the world is filled with generous, kind people. I was cognizant of diverse cultures. My initial assumptions were often wrong. For example, hand gestures have different meanings in many countries, and what is innocuous in one place is offensive elsewhere. In parts of Asia, the placement of my feet, depending on location or position, was an insult.

The first hurdle to overcome in international travel is generally language. Today, English is the language used for air traffic controllers and for a conversation between German and French tourists who meet in Spain. There are more countries with English as a second language, and some native English speakers are hesitant to learn a foreign language. In my world travels in the '60s and '70s, this was not the case. Although today, as I struggle to communicate in a foreign language, my efforts are rewarded. Total immersion into a culture and language is priceless.

The answer for my survival on a number of occasions is mystifying, yet I overcame monumental problems throughout my life. I did not focus solely on the positive times in this book because there are valuable lessons from both. Life offers the highest of highs and the lowest of lows. The happy-go-lucky traveler has the brightest and darkest days. As the world evolves, so do I.

I was unaware my dilemma had a name—PTSD—until I was 47 years old. I was given a 35% chance of survival, with a 10% chance of successful relationships. The odds were not in my favor. Oh, the joy of proving the pundits wrong is the greatest satisfaction. My beloved wife Jill was incredibly supportive as I collected my thoughts and memories to share with you.

Saviors appeared when I was stranded, whether it was a talking bush, or sleeping in a comfortable one. The wise old man who said, "Never give up or give an inch," offered sound advice, and help is only one question away.

The crucial aspect of winning the rest of one's life is plainly the fundamentals of achieving happiness one molecule at a time. It may sound simplistic, but one small shift makes all the difference in the journey from the cradle to the grave.

Life is short, I was told as a youngster. My elders advised me to value my youth and have fun because time and life pass rapidly. This was the best advice of my life from both a healing and gratification perspective. Roads are paths to the next adventure.

As I recall the days in the classroom, staring at the teacher's globe from my desk, exploring the world proved dreams come true. This elixir was the perfect prescription for mending my broken spirit.

Other travelers mentioned the addictive qualities of the open road, and what a lovely addiction it is. I traveled the world when barely out of my teens, and my adventures were priceless lessons in life. My travels were during the period when airfares were more expensive, and immediacy of communication was unimportant. I relied mainly on word of mouth through the backpackers' grapevine.

There are differences between traveling five decades ago and now, but some similarities never change. My primary guideline was to master traveling on a tight budget. I chose to meet the enormity of this challenge and accomplished this by compartmentalizing each step of the journey. This effective tactic translates to guaranteeing the success of any endeavor.

Working around the world is not for everyone although it was the most valuable education for me. Traveling with funds and having a place to stay also affords a similar outcome. Whichever option is chosen, a meaningful odyssey is in store.

I traveled with bits and pieces of information, without maps or a full grasp of my surroundings. There were many serendipitous moments. The strangers who yelled from out of the blue recommending this restaurant or that neighborhood—their suggestions were gold when I was lost in a fog. It was seamless to the extent that it was overlooked how the universe supported my endeavors at the time. Murphy's Law was reversed at the most opportune moments.

Today, I prefer to avoid the temptation of searching online for tourist information because this may stifle serendipity. Discovery is my favorite component of traveling. The best recipe for success on the road is when all the elements coalesce to create a delicious dessert. The lessons from cooking and traveling are comparable.

Each ingredient, spice, and flavor which enhances cooking is the same with travel. The characteristic of each interaction with individuals around the world creates the special sauce for unbelievable times. The world is a magnificent place. Perhaps a spark of inspiration has been lit for you to embark on your own journey.

I'll leave things there; that will do. I finished writing, and I'll edit tomorrow. The recollections, for the most part, were spectacular.

Many of my generation only traveled once and in one direction, overseas to a war from which they never returned. Yes, I had my misfortunes, disappointments, and losses, but I survived to share my exploits.

So where to next? Where will it be? Deciding where to go for my next trip is almost as much fun as visiting these exotic locales. I launch Google Earth on my computer and zoom out until I see our planet from space. With a flick of my finger on the mouse, it spins and where will it stop? Somewhere I've been before or someplace new? Zoom in now, Ron and see where you might go.

It's time for music. What will it be? I've created a playlist of all the songs to complement my adventures, but it's time for something else. My finger dances across the vinyl albums I still play today and pauses on the letter C. That will do.

I slide the record from the sleeve, wipe it carefully, and rest it on the turntable. Canned Heat '70 Concert - Recorded Live in Europe. As the first track plays, I browse the playlist. Track four is on deck, and I smile. A medley of Back Out on the Road and On the Road Again.

Made in the USA
Columbia, SC
20 December 2023

29030624R00152